# THE COASTS OF WALES

# The Coasts of Wales

H. L. V. Fletcher

*Illustrated and with map*

ROBERT HALE · LONDON

Robert Hale & Company,
63 Old Brompton Road,
London, S.W.7.

Printed and bound in Great Britain by
C. Tinling & Co. Ltd., London and Prescot.

# CONTENTS

# ILLUSTRATIONS

# PICTURE SOURCES

I wish to thank Llandudno Town Council for the illustration of the Great Orme; Colwyn Bay Town Council for the view of Colwyn Bay; Lord Longford, Constable of Rhuddlan Castle, and The Ministry of Public Building and Works for the view of the castle (Crown copyright); and Chester City Council for the view of salmon fishing boats. The other photographs were taken specially for this volume.

H.L.V.F.

## ACKNOWLEDGEMENTS

I WOULD like to thank everybody who has helped me in any way in the writing of this book. While I have not prepared a formal bibliography I am very conscious of the debt I owe to so many writers who have been over the ground before me. I have read and learned from so many: Giraldus Cambrensis, John Leland, George Borrow, Thomas Pennant, Sabine Baring-Gould, A. G. Bradley and many others. I have learned something from each, and I hope the quotations from their books may persuade others to open them again.

Once again I am happy to thank our Radnorshire librarian, Mr. C. W. Newman and his staff, who have taken so much trouble to help me and find me the books I wanted.

H.L.V.F.

*Llandrindod Wells*

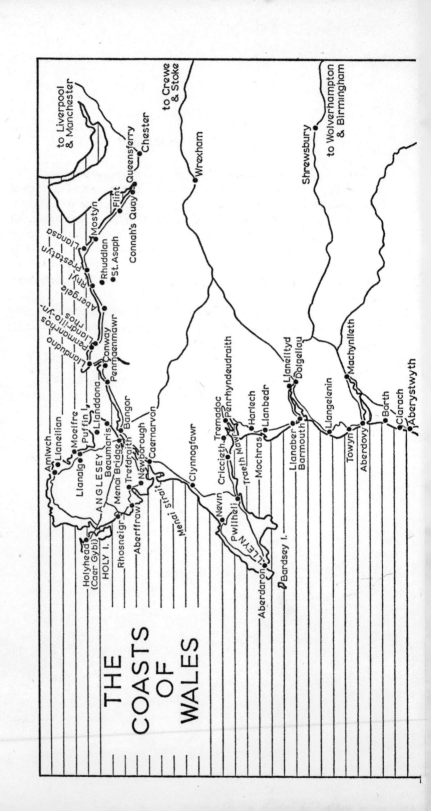

THE COASTS OF WALES

to Birmingham

to Worcester

Hereford

to Gloucester

Bishton
Chepstow
Caerwent
Portskewett
Magor Undy Caldicot
Redwick
Whitson

Caerleon
Newport
Goldcliff

Cardiff
Penarth
Lavernock
Barry

Aberthaw
Penmark
St. Athan
Llantwit Major
St. Donats

Port Talbot
Neath
Margam
Kenfig
Nottage
Porthcawl
Dunraven

Swansea
Loughor
Mumbles

Burry Port
Llanelli

Llanstephan
Ferryside
Kidwelly
Laugharne

Rhossili

Llanon
Aberaeron
Aberarth
New Quay
Llangranog
Aberporth

Lampeter

Carmarthen
Abergwili

Verwick

Amroth
Marros
Pendine
Saundersfoot
Tenby
Penally
Caldy I.
Lydstep Haven
Manorbier

Mynydd
Prescelly

Fishguard

Solva

Bishop &
Clarks
Ramsey

Mynydd Prescelly
Haverfordwest

Skomer
Skokholm
Marloes
Dale
Angle
St. Ishmael's
Milford
Haven
Stapeside
Lamphey

0        20
Miles
0

# CHAPTER I

## MONMOUTH TO NEWPORT

THE last time I was in South Monmouthshire the hawthorn was in full flower. The sun was strong and the heady scent from white-laden trees came through the open windows of the car, and very pleasant and sweet and pastoral everything was. You couldn't see very far—you can't in that part of the world when trees and hedges are in leaf—and we went sedately through the quiet lanes—a very good job they are quiet for width is not one of their virtues—through little villages, Roggiett and Undy, Magor and Bishton, past quiet cottages and small churches. The road winds a good deal in places, and most of the ways we took were bordered by deep ditches—reens they call them, or is it rhines?—that drain this low, level land. Now that was not so good for my ancient car is wide and likes room to spread itself. If I met anything, somebody would have to back—might have to back a long way, and I could see myself with a few tons of car half in half out of one of the rhines. There were farm entrances where you were implored or ordered not to park, and occasionally a notice that said we were on our way to the sea-wall (which we never reached anyhow); we passed a pub, a farm, a church. No traffic to speak of; a lark singing; always the scent of hawthorn. It seemed as quiet a place as you would find anywhere in the country. And so it was.

I have a feeling it may remain like that for a very long time. There is no seaside resort to draw the people and the traffic. I don't say nobody ever goes down for a picnic, and Olive Phillips in her *Monmouthshire* makes it clear that they went quite frequently in summer (gargantuan picnics those were, too), but it was, I think, before the days when everyone had a car. Now they hare along on the motorway as fast as they can to Barry or Porthcawl. So if you want peace and quiet try Monmouthshire south of the motorway. The modern motorways have many virtues—and as a means of getting from one place to another I'm all for them. It may be that a future age, when some other means of communication has taken the place of the ones we have now, will see real beauty and grace in their smooth curves and clean lines. And, fair play to them, they do have points in their favour, and the aforementioned help in making a tedious journey with speed (I being old and square enough to consider 70 m.p.h. as speed!) is one.

But I am getting away from my point, which is that, for relaxed peace and quietness, the Monmouthshire coast lanes are going to take some equalling for many years to come. Above the motorway, I mean north of it, are the industrial valleys and the great and ancient Forest of Wentwood; and away from the valleys, and Aberdare and Abergavenny and Ebbw Vale and Pontypool, there are villages and woods, castles and lovely stately houses, and all that makes a countryside pleasant, including peace, for if you wander north you will come to the quiet valleys of the Black Mountains and the loneliness to which you have to be born to be able to live in it. At any rate it was too isolated for the monks who settled at Llanthony, or for the would-be monks who could not stay when their leader, Father Ignatius, had died, or for Eric Gill and the artists who thought they had found Paradise and realised a little late that Paradise, in contrast to the other place, could be, in winter anyhow, a mighty cold spot.

But I stay away too long from where I (at the moment and in this book) should remain: the coast.

It suddenly strikes me—how wide is a coast? Am I to walk along the water's edge and never leave it. Must I be like the Lady of Shallot in her tower, under a curse if I so much as lift my eyes to what there is beyond? No, indeed, I shall go where I like. I ask a friend as I write, how wide is a coast, and very cleverly he says that I am at liberty to stray up any valley as far as the tidal waters go. That's quite smart, but suppose round the next bend there is a lovely village, or an ancient church or an old friend I haven't seen for years?

I knew a rich man once—I haven't known many of those, though I hear they are around still—and he married a young wife, and when, in his bored way, he would say, what are we going to do now, she'd reply, Leave it to me, Joe, leave it all to me (which, in case you think they were a horrid pair, was their private joke).

Anyhow, literally or metaphorically, it was good advice. I pass it on.

Monmouthshire, between motorway and sea is as good a place to get lost in as you could find—in summer. I must stress that: *in summer*, with the hawthorn out or the wild roses, and the birds singing. But this can, too, be a desolate place: too quiet, too empty, too deserted. When the leaves are off the trees and the sky is grey and there is a cold south-wester blowing off the sea, or, perhaps worse, not even the wind for company, but a mist that you can't see through for twenty yards, then the north bank of the Severn Estuary can be a very dreary place indeed. You cannot see far, and the damp seems to get right into your bones. It is very quiet; the cottage doors are shut, and the garden flowers have faded long since. The little churches are grim and lonely with only the ghosts of the centuries for company; the lanes seem narrower than ever they were when the sun shone, and the rhines deeper and much too full of water. This is the lonely land. I feel it should have capitals: The Lonely Land.

Of course it is not as bad as that; but come in summer if you can—and even then choose a day when the sun is shining.

And what of the sea. Well the sea you may, to make a picturesque phrase, call the Severn Sea. That has a pleasant alliterative sound, but the Severn river it is (with a good bit of Wye as well), and it goes past (on the ebb) swirling and eddying with a quiet, mind-your-own-business sort of song that you can hear if you will listen carefully. It is bringing down a good bit of mud from a dozen Welsh and English counties, and this it leaves between high and low water, so that, once the tide is out, in many parts there is some sand above high-water mark, but mostly a lot of mud below it. As you come down from Chepstow, say at Portskewett, there is not exactly cliff, but quite a fair drop from land to sand, but as you get further down this levels out and there is so little rise that a high tide can push the water into the rhines and on occasion, with wind and tide unfavourable, has pushed it a good deal above them—with disastrous results.

Of course, with so much deposit—and the Wye does its share, though Severn has most of the blame—the channel is subject to change. Mud banks and sand banks are built up, but are liable—over long periods of time anyhow—to be found in some other place than you expect them. Heavy shipping, of course, what there is of it still so far up (fair-sized boats can still go to Gloucester) moves well out in mid-channel. Those of moderate draught treat the coast with respect, and really small boating is not common.

There was a ferry once at Portskewett, and close by a reef called the Englishmen's Stones. There is a tradition that Charles I was ferried across here from Monmouthshire to Gloucestershire, and then on his return the ferrymen found sixty of Cromwell's troops who were pursuing the king. They made him help the pursuit by ferrying them across but he took them to the Englishmen's Stones, put them off there, saying that was the limit to which he could take the ferryboat. He then pulled out into the Channel again and watched them drown as the tide rose. As a result the ferry rights were taken away.

There is a fair amount of industry, factories, cement-making and so on around Portskewett, and, as there must be where there is industry, a good deal of building, good, indifferent and poor. But none of the factory districts have spread far, and you soon hear more seabirds than hooters, more sea-sirens (if your ears are tuned to such music) than factory sirens. At one time there were other industries, and within sight of St. Tecla's Island—or Treacle Island, if you would prefer the corruption—I have looked down into the deep mud that the river has deposited in an old shipyard. No hammers ring now, and I expect the little boats they built have long ago rotted on some far-away beach into decent decay.

Chepstow is the sort of town I like. Mind I've nothing against Cardiff or Swansea or the rowdy jollity of Porthcawl. But up-hill-and-down-dale Chepstow is just big enough to be a town and just small enough to notice you. You don't live here, and they find where you *do* live, and somebody is *sure* to know somebody *you* know, were talking to only a week ago. With luck somebody actually knows somebody who lived where you used to live. This sort of thing warms you up, makes you feel among friends, so that one of you, if not both, comes out with that well-worn statement that the world is a small place. So it is too (never mind clichés), and a very good thing because the universe outside it is big enough in all conscience.

Chepstow Castle, one of the best-preserved along the border, you feel should dominate the town, but it does not for they tucked it on a rise down above the Wye. That at least gave very good defence on most of a couple of sides, the river doing one of its famous curves here. There is a good little bridge with white Wye cliffs on the other shore, but I suppose they'll be pulling it down one of these days to give that holy cow, traffic, more space to threaten you and deafen

Allteryn—Newport

you and poison you. Different from the time they were repairing it—oh, it was a long time ago; it's one of the stories they told me—when there was about the width of one narrow plank left and a horseman came into town on his horse. A good surefooted horse, too, for it found its way in the dark and brought its master across safely. When they showed him the next day how near they had been to falling into the Wye, he fainted!

He was luckier than the Radnorshire horseman whose mare took him over almost depthless Llyngwyn in a snowstorm when the lake was frozen. When he found out how close he had been to the Styx he dropped dead from shock.

History repeats itself: so do the best stories!

Perhaps they were a bit careless about bridges in this part of the world because I suddenly call to mind another bridge story I heard. And, though it was some two centuries ago, the details were all included. Nothing vague like "there used to be a chap living round here. . . ."

No indeed! There was, up to the late eighteenth century, a wooden bridge over the Usk at Caerleon. On one side lived a man by the name of Williams. On the other was an inn. Williams spent more time in the inn than he did at home. Mrs. Williams was very cross about it. One night there was a bad storm. The Usk rose; the bridge groaned and creaked. At last Mrs. Williams decided to fetch her husband home. She lit a lantern to show her the way. When she got to the bridge it was protesting so much she was almost afraid to cross. But she did. Or she started to. When she was half way across, the bridge broke away in the force of the flood and went sailing down river. Williams, having heard his wife's screams, came to the inn door. By the light of her lantern he saw her start off on what was undoubtedly her last voyage.

"What a good job as I wasn't on it!" he exclaimed as he went back to his beer.

Miraculously, the bridge did not break up. It went tearing down, Mrs. Williams screaming, her lantern flickering its way over the waters like a glow-worm in a raining gutter. Her strange craft ought to have smashed up on Newport Bridge, but her luck held and she shot through one of the arches. Below the bridge lay the Plymouth ship *The Hawk*, and the crew, who had heard the woman's screams and saw her light, put out a boat and rescued her. When the captain heard her story he hired a chaise for her and sent her back to

Elizabethan (Magistrate's) House, St. Nicholas, Glamorgan
The Old Smuggler's Inn at Llantwit Major

B

Caerleon. And there she waited, "nursing her wrath to keep it warm".

When the river went down next day one of her friends ferried Williams home. And then—for him—the storm broke out again.

The story seemed, to me, a sort of "Tam o' Shanter" in reverse. But alas, though south Monmouthshire has had its minor poets and Newport one very good one (of whom more later), there wasn't a Burns among them.

Chepstow Castle was a famous strongpoint in the long Anglo-Welsh struggle, and inside its walls sad events have had sad endings. But Jeremy Taylor (*Holy Living* and *Holy Dying*) survived to become a bishop; and Henry Marten, who was one of those who signed Charles I's death warrant, had, for a state prisoner, a very tolerable twenty years of imprisonment, with his family round him and liberty, on occasions at least, to visit friends outside. He was 78 when he died, and then they buried him near the altar in St. Mary's Church (which still has much Norman architecture), though a later parson thought he was not quite saintly enough for so privileged a place and had him re-buried further down the chancel, where you can still read the epitaph he composed for himself.

But strong castles were for the times when a strong wall had to be climbed or breached. After the Civil War and one last disastrous defeat for the King's men it was a fortress no longer. I suspect that, like other castles, it is a pleasanter place as a ruin than it ever was as a Marcher lord's headquarters.

From Chepstow you can tear up the motorway to Newport or you can go by way of the lanes through the marshes or over the levels. Between the latter there is not much difference except the one of title. The land is low, and the Severn swirls by moodily. Once, you may be told, it was a great place for wrecking and for smuggling. But they will tell you that all round the coast from the Wye to the Dee. And indeed, on a darkening evening with grey skies and a flock of oyster-catchers mewing plaintively as they skim the waves, you can imagine either of these primitive and sometimes profitable occupations being carried on. But what is the truth of it all? Well, the coast of Wales is a long trek. Earl Harold is said to have carved on stones where he went: *Here Harold conquered*, but I have no ambition to keep repeating *Here were smugglers* every place I stop.

Leave the wrecking out a moment—it never was romantic, and neither was it in general as evil as it has been painted. I know a little about it in its more innocent aspects, and later I want to say more about it, but one thing at a time, as Humphrey Watt's dog said when he started a rabbit and a hare together. (That's a Pembrokeshire story, by the way, so it is not due yet. But Humphrey put down his scythe blade upwards, the dog sliced itself down the middle and one half caught the rabbit, the other the hare.)

To get the moral issue clear first, I do not think that, in principle, most people have much conscientious objection to smuggling. Smuggling on the large scale, where it is just a money-making racket—yes. Fifty thousand Swiss watches or cameras, or a fortune in cigarettes, or a few thousand pounds' worth of drugs: that is just money-grubbing at everybody's expense, and nobody sheds tears when the culprits are caught. But the odd bottle of brandy or scent, the few extra cigars, the watch, the camera or pair of field-glasses— that is breaking the rules, and rules, so they say, are there to be broken. Not all wrong-doing is sin, and most consciences go untroubled after getting the better of the Customs people. And let me say, in case this makes me suspect, that I don't think I've ever smuggled so much as a half-bottle of table wine. Not that *my* conscience is more tender than anybody else's: I'm just not brave enough, and I'd feel an awful fool if I did smuggle and were caught.

But the smuggling of old has become in retrospect a romantic business.

Five and twenty ponies
Trotting through the dark—
Brandy for the Parson,
'Baccy for the Clerk.

The critics may say what they like about Kipling; he knew his business.

Watch the wall, my darling, while the Gentlemen go by.

The dark nights, the muffled pony hoofbeats, the stuff covered with straw in the outhouse, the outwitted preventive officers . . . sounds exciting good-old-days material.

Now I would not debunk a good fairy story for anything but what is the truth of it? Well, to start with as I work it out, if all the stuff was smuggled on these lonely coasts they say there was, all legitimate trade would have died right out. There just wouldn't be room in the country to hold all the brandy that *might* have been smuggled on the shores of the Welsh sea-coast counties.

The Preventive Officers weren't all such awful fools. The coast-guards—their equivalent when I was a youngster—certainly were not. They used to say that you couldn't get so much as a plank out of the sea in Carmarthen Bay without the Tenby coastguard knowing about it. Not that he ever followed up bits and pieces as trifling as that—but he *knew*!

A ship-owner who got caught smuggling could lose a lot more than he gained. His vessel could be confiscated.

To smuggle on a worthwhile scale needed a lot of organisation. Much more and much more cleverly planned than local idlers or longshoremen could manage. You'd have to allow for tides, weather and a whole jigsaw of local conditions to be successful half the time.

And finally: for over half a century my home was on a quiet, easy, currentless coast; sandy beaches at low tide; pebble ridges at the full. In decent weather you could have run boats in, nine nights out of ten without the least danger of running the risk of that sharp-eyed chap on Tenby Castle Hill getting suspicious. And never in all the time I lived there, or when I still visit it, have I heard anything about smuggling, or of any places where it went on. And if you think, of course I wouldn't hear about secrets like that, then all I can say is you don't know what life in a small village was like.

We knew how to keep our mouths shut; we didn't tell everything we knew to strangers; but there weren't any such things as secrets!

I am not saying no smuggling ever went on, but when it did it was, as it is now, big business and financed by men already rich. Occasionally, but only occasionally by a squire who owned coast property. And there were such characters as the Knights of Cardiff, Marisco of Lundy and Cruel Coppinger of Hartland on the Devon coast. But these were pirates, unscrupulous and savage as wolves. No doubt there was, here and there a bit of 'bacca and a drop of brandy on which duty had not been paid. I've had a hint that the trade has not *completely* become obsolete. But it's small beer now.

My own belief is it always was.

St. Paul said we should not encourage things "whereby thy brother stumbleth, or is offended, or made weak", so I hope nothing I have written will be considered as encouragement to try a little duty-dodging on the side.

Portskewett seems to be much built-up now. In ancient Welsh writings it was described as one of the three chief harbours of Wales, which, however you look at it, sounds a slight exaggeration. What

does seem certain is that there was once a ferry from the English
side, and that was part of the Roman way from England to South
Wales. There are traces of Roman Buildings in the neighbourhood,
and at nearby Sudbrook all sorts of relics were found, some dating
back to the Iron Age. The church at Portskewett contains much
Norman work, and there are interesting traces of Tudor alterations.
For some odd reason the village stocks were taken to Chepstow.

"They needed 'em more than us", said one Portskewett worthy.

There always was a ferry at Black Rock, not a bad place for a
picnic, by the way, as the Severn shore goes, but there are some
quite frightening currents apparent at certain periods of the tide.
I'd hate to go swimming there. At Sudbrook they made the Severn
Tunnel. I'm no engineer, and I suppose they *did* pick the best spot,
but I was told there is a depth of nearly sixty feet of water and the
tunnel had to go thirty feet below that. Even then they ran into
unexpected trouble. The work was started in 1873 and went on well
until 1879 when suddenly the tunnel was flooded. They thought at
first that this was Severn water, but it was not. They had touched
a land spring, and it was no mere trickle either. Shafts were flooded
to a great depth, a pumping shaft had to be made to pump out the
water, and, so far as I know, it is still pumped out, over 10 million
gallons a day I've been told. It was 1887 before the tunnel was
completed.

I'm not, I repeat, an engineer, and I listen respectfully to the tales
I am told. But sometimes I wonder if the right hand knows what
the left hand doeth (or knoweth). I wrote above what I was told:
that there is sixty-foot depth of water in the Channel and that the
tunnel went thirty feet below that. Total: ninety feet. Yet another
yarn was that when the great spring broke in shafts were flooded to
a depth of 150 feet. Counting from sea level I can't quite see where
that other sixty feet of water stood. So if you come across some daft
sets of figures occasionally don't *always* blame me!

Caldicot for example. It is a good Welsh mile west of Portskewett
and well worth visiting for a sight of its fine old castle. But on the
Ordnance map Caldicot Level—the flat coastal plain—is miles on
to the west around Redwick and Whitson. Of course, as I have said
already, it is all flat land, but I'm never quite sure why they called
it the *Caldicot* Level when Magor, with its church so imposing that
they called it the Cathedral of the Moors, is so much more central.
Magor, too, has many important historical associations. Cadwalader,

the last Welsh king of Britain founded the church in the seventh century, and in the thirteenth it was associated with (or belonged to) an Italian convent and later became part of the possessions of Tintern Abbey. For a thousand years history touched the villages of the moors and levels only slightly, but Magor was not unknown outside Gwent.

Between Roggiett, where the Severn Tunnel starts its gentle slide downwards, and Magor, is Undy, whose chief claim to fame is that more than half its acreage is foreshore.

Only a short distance north of Caldicot are the ruins of the old Roman town of Caerwent. Caerwent has been dwarfed somewhat in antiquarian interest by the fact that Caerleon, one of the really famous Roman stations lay only some ten miles or less to the west, but, though they say the population can have been only a few thousands, it must have been a place of some importance, as you may judge by the uncovered and restored town wall about 500 yards in length. Some say it was the administrative centre for the west of Roman Britain, though I am not told what is the authority for this statement. The place covered some fifty acres, had four gates, and inside there was a forum, a basilica, a temple, a public bath and an amphitheatre. All these in addition to the usual houses, shops, inns and so on. Once the empire went into decline Caerwent declined also, and in the following centuries was never more than a small Celtic settlement round the little monastery founded by St. Tathan. Borrow said it was "a poor desolate place consisting of a few old-fashioned houses and a strange-looking delapidated church". Actually it is a very pleasant spot.

At Caerwent are traces of a number of cultures: the Iron Age; the well-planned Roman city; the medieval town. But it always seems to me that there is little reliable information about the Roman occupation, colonisation—call it what you will—of Britain. The battles we know about, the Boadiceas, the Caratacuses; there are traces of the buildings; the roads still run out in all directions and we can stand on the northern protective walls that run across the country.

But what did go on? And *why*, when the master race left, did so many lovely towns, so many fine houses, stay empty and fall into decay. Why didn't the Ancient Britons move in eagerly. I can only touch on the fringes of history, and I realise very well that there are exceptions—London and Chester for example—and that to the expert I must appear to be making sweeping statements that sound uncommonly like the buzzing of bees in my own bonnet. But, just as a simple example, take my own little corner of Radnorshire.

The Romans built a fortress, a small settlement perhaps, at Castell Collen. It was fortified, it was a good defensive position, it lay on a road that crossed the best and most usable ford on the Ithon (below what we now call Lover's Leap). Castell Collen had everything in its favour to grow into the chief local town. Yet the town (village then) grew up a mile and more away, and the walls of Castell Collen, like those of a greater city, came tumbling down.

This avoidance of the fine Roman cities took place everywhere. Hardly in any place did the Britons move in, occupy, build, improve. Roman Britain was succeeded by a dark age, and we don't know much about it, only that fine cities decayed, the houses fell down, the baths were unbathed in, the amphitheatres were silent. This had been no brief occupation, mind; it had lasted between 300 and 400 years, yet Caernarvon grew up apart from Segontium, Hereford some miles from Kentchurch. And so everywhere.

Nationalism? Resentment? Hatred of a regime that at worst was never oppressive? Fear of a return? Superstition? Perhaps some clever Roman historian knows the simple answer. Or perhaps there is not one. And a supposition that the British did live in Roman luxury until the barbarians began to arrive, is not, for me, satisfactory.

Well, this is one of my own bees: let it buzz!

A few miles further west was Caerleon. Caerwent was largely an administrative centre; Caerleon was a fortress garrisoned by the Second Legion, one of the more notable Roman regiments. There were about 6,000 men, and when Wales was put into some sort of order many of the legionaries went north to help in the building of Hadrian's Wall. But the Welshmen became rebellious again and in the early third century Caerleon seems to have become an important military centre once more.

It was one of those cities in which the cult of the goddess Diana was the principal religion. Yet not the only one, for there is a tradition that two Christian saints, Julius and Aaron, were put to death there in the late third century. This is a little more than interesting because the very early arrival of the Christian religion in Wales, centuries before Augustine's arrival in England, is well-known, though nobody seems able to guess with much certainty

how or where or when it arrived. There is another legend that Saint
Peter and Saint Paul came as missionaries and penetrated north to
the borders of Breconshire and west at least as far as the Tawe
Valley. That is not impossible: the galleys of Tyre and Sidon had
reached Cornwall long before their time; and they had both stirred
things up well in many of the larger cities of the eastern Mediter-
ranean and could have been glad to find new fields to work in. Paul
would hardly have enjoyed Caerleon though. The cult of Diana had
given him a lively time at Ephesus.*

For my own part, without ambition to be regarded as a serious
and dead-accurate historian, I think Christianity came to these parts
very early. It may have been brought by a few Roman converts, but
I don't see why it should not have been introduced by some of the
first Jewish Christians themselves. When the Romans under Titus
flattened Palestine to put down the rebellion in the sixties A.D.,
they destroyed Jerusalem, after one of the most famous sieges in
history. Such Jews as were fortunate enough to escape death or
slavery were dispersed all over the face of the earth. There is evidence
that some of them got as far as north China, a most unlikely part for
settlers in those times (or later), so it seems reasonable to expect that
some would come west, especially to parts that the Romans had
pacified. They could still enjoy the benefits of a civilisation they
were used to, but avoid the savage cruelty under which their friends
were suffering in Rome.

I don't know how long through history names can persist, but in
South Wales there is a big proportion of Jewish ones: Isaacs and
Moses; Jacobs and Samuels; Samsons and Abrahams and Absoloms;
practically every Old Testament name can be heard as a Welsh
surname. Mixed up in the variety of faces and shapes of heads,
there can be seen quite a few dark eastern-type profiles also (the
handsome ones, of course!). And there is the fervid love of music
and the quick preoccupation with religion; the lack of interest in
the graphic arts (*Thou shalt not make unto thyself any graven image*)
and the love of poetry (not always good poetry, though). So sometimes I imagine small bands of the earliest Christians arriving at the
outskirts of the Roman Empire—and then pushing on a bit beyond
it. South Wales always was hospitable.

Thomas Richards who compiled a Welsh-English Dictionary in
1753 says, "It hath been observed, that our language hath not a great

* Acts 19: 23–41.

many Marks of the original Simplicity of the Hebrew but that a
vast Number of Words are found therein, that either exactly agree
with, or may be very naturally derived from that Mother-language
of Mankind."

Another personal bee buzzing, of course!

So Caerleon rose and Caerleon fell. Yet not so quickly, for in the
late twelfth century Giraldus said,

> Many vestiges of its former splendour may yet be seen; immense palaces,
> formerly ornamented with gilded roofs, in imitation of Roman magnificence,
> inasmuch as they were first raised by the Roman princes, and embellished with
> splendid buildings; a tower of prodigious size, remarkable hot baths, relics
> of temples, and theatres, all enclosed within fine walls, parts of which remain
> standing. You will find on all sides, both within and without the circuit of
> the walls, subterraneous buildings, aqueducts, underground passages; and
> what I think worthy of notice, stoves contrived with wonderful art, to transmit
> the heat insensibly through narrow tubes passing up the side walls.

Caerleon, too, was the birthplace of the Arthurian legend. That
Arthur was a British hero there is little doubt; that he was a king is
likely—but, alas, the knights in shining armour and the lovely
damsels come from the imagination of the unreliable Geoffrey of
Monmouth, though he must surely have had *some* grounds on which
to base the greatest hero-lore in Europe. Other writers did their
share, notably Sir Thomas Malory; then, nearer our own times,
Tennyson was so enchanted by the music he sang that he came to
Caerleon for the atmosphere and for inspiration. "The Usk murmurs
by the windows, and I sit like King Arthur at Caerleon."

So he put the seal of his cadences on the legends that had been
accumulating for centuries. But what magnificent legends!

Tennyson is despised now by the cleverest critics. No doubt the
poets they praise are better than he was: they say so, and they should
know. But who now will write our fairy stories for us?

So Caerleon fell down, and Newport grew up, and the galleys no
longer went up-river to the Roman city. A bridge was built, and the
ships stayed. In time the coal and iron industries flourished in north
Glamorgan and north Monmouth, and the town grew into one of
the largest and most important cities on the coasts of the Bristol
Channel. But when Newport began to flourish while Caerleon fell
into decline, all that was far in the future.

There was a castle at Newport, but less of that remains than the
Roman fortress. It never recovered from being sacked by Owain

Glyndwr in 1402, though there was some attempt to put it into order as a Royalist strongpoint during the Civil War. The most interesting building is the cathedral church of St. Woolos on Stow Hill, with a grand tower that can be seen from all down the Bristol Channel. It grew from a tiny church built by St. Woolos (Gwynllyw in Welsh) in the sixth century; it was plundered by Irish, destroyed by Danes and, for good measure, by any local Welsh prince who happened to be on the warpath. The monks of St. Peter's, Gloucester, at last gave it form and shape and strength, and it survived Glyndwr. Later Jasper Tudor, son of Owain Tudor and Henry V's widow, Catherine, had the tower built. There is still some of the finest Norman church architecture to be found in South Wales in St. Woolos.

Some of the Chartists who lost their lives in the 1839 riots are buried in the churchyard. The Newport riots are history. It is strange to reflect that much the Chartists agitated for—manhood suffrage, votes by ballot, payment for Members of Parliament—are now looked on as automatic democratic rights, but the methods by which they tried to get them, and the leadership that brought them to disaster, do appear, to say the least, slightly naive.

Discontent with social conditions was at boiling point in the northern industrial valleys. Under the leadership of William Jones of Pontypool, Zephaniah Williams of Nant-y-glo and John Frost, ex-mayor of Newport, the Chartists were to march on Newport and sieze the town. After that, rebellion would break out in the country, the reforms would be made, and all would be well.

Of course all never was well. The rebels entered Newport on 4th November 1839, attacked the Westgate Hotel, where some soldiers had taken up position, were fired on . . . and the rebellion died, almost before it had started; and so came the new graves in St. Woolos' churchyard. About fourteen men were killed, something like fifty wounded.

The three leaders were tried on a charge of high treason and condemned to death. The sentence was commuted to life trans-portation, and they were sent to Tasmania. In 1854 they were pardoned, and Frost came home and died at Stapleton near Bristol in 1877. For what is generally thought of as a harsh unenlightened age—the 1840s—they were more gently handled than one might have expected. Their cause was just; their methods of trying to achieve it simple, if not downright foolish. I suppose that sums up many of us.

W. H. Davies was born in Newport in 1871 at Church House Tavern, which was kept by his Cornish grandfather who had once been a sea-captain. Davies started work as a picture-frame maker but gave that up to become a tramp and, by his own description, "Super Tramp". He spent some years in America, came home, went to Canada and then lost his right leg in an accident while 'riding the rods', which means stealing rides on the under-carriages of railway trains, surely the most uncomfortable form of free transport ever discovered. Down-and-out, he came back to England, went on the road again, and, an unusual occupation for a tramp, wrote poetry. He even, still more unusual, got some published, and when it looked like being a failure took to dropping copies through the letter boxes of distinguished authors, asking them either to buy them or return them. A number of writers recognised the quality of the poetry, the most-quoted example being Bernard Shaw, and, with their help, Davies won recognition, an income and eventually fame. He has told his own story in his *Autobiography of a Super Tramp*. Interesting though this is, his prose has not the high quality of his poems, some of which are comparable to the finest lyrical poetry in the language. Even hackneyed repetition has failed to spoil them, and there is still pleasure in reading:

> What is this life if, full of care,
> We have no time to stand and stare.

W. H. Davies died in September 1940. There is, or was if the town planners have not knocked it down, a plaque on the house in which he was born.

Catastrophes are like people: Some as it is written in Ecclesiasticus are "as though they had never been"; others cannot be forgotten.

The Great Flood of south Monmouthshire is among the latter. It happened on 20th January 1606, and a worse day for a flood (if any could be *much* worse than another) than a cold one in winter can hardly be imagined.

In those pre-newspaper days only the most notable events went on record. The flood was one, and a broadsheet was published giving an account. There is no reason to suppose that those early journalists were any more unreliable than those of the present day, and they certainly wrote as well:

> About nine of the clock in the morning, the same being most fairly and brightly spread, many of the inhabitants prepared themselves to their affairs.

Then they might see afar off huge and mighty hills of water tumbling over one another as if the greatest mountains in the world had overwhelmed the low villages and marshy grounds. Sometimes it dazzled many of the spectators that they imagined it had been some fog or mist coming with great swiftness towards them, and with such a smoke as if mountains were all on fire, and to the view of some it seemed as if millions of thousands of arrows had been shot forth all at one time. So violent and swift were the outrageous waves that in less than five hours space most part of those counties (especially the places that lay low) were all overflown, and many hundreds of people, men, women and children, were quite devoured; nay, more, the farmers and husbandmen and shepherds might behold their goodly flocks swimming upon the waters—dead.

There was a primitive little woodcut as illustration, as simple as the picture to a nursery rhyme. The roof of a church sticks up out of the water. Men, or boys, one naked (on a January morning!), cling to a couple of trees; a man wearing his tall steeple hat sits on a roof; animals and human beings swim in the water. All rather quaint and quite failing to depict the sheer misery and horror of the occasion —which may be just as well.

The flood affected an area some twenty-four miles long and about four miles wide. Twenty-six parishes suffered; about 2,000 people lost their lives, and the damage to property was thought to be near £100,000. The local gentry did noble relief work. They carted boats to the area without losing any time, or the loss of life might have been greater.

There are still local reminders: a stone in the chancel of Peterstone church marks the level to which the water rose; while at Goldcliff, nearly two miles from the sea, there was three feet of water in the church, and the churchwardens had an account of the catastrophe engraved on a brass plate:

1606

On the XX day of January even as it came to pas it pleased God the flud did flow to the edge of this same bras and in this parish theare was lost 5000 and od pownds besides, XXII people was in this parish drown.

Goldclif { John Wilkins of Pil Rew and
William Tap Church Wardens.

1609

There was no poet to do for the Marshes what Jean Ingelow did for the Lincolnshire Flood of 1571:

Then banks came down with ruin and rout—
Then beaten foam flew round about—
Then all the mighty floods were out.

.     .     .     .     .

The feet had hardly time to flee
Before it broke against the knee,
And all the world was in the sea.

The Romans had built a sea wall to protect the low-lying parts of this land. After the Great Flood it was repaired and strengthened again.

Always *after*!

CHAPTER 2

# CARDIFF TO GOWER

ONE day should be exactly like another: but it never is. If you are unconscious or sleeping, Monday might be no different from Friday, but to those of us who are awake and go about our affairs it is very different indeed. So, land being land and sea being sea, one shore should be very like the next: but again it never is. Nobody could confuse the muddy Severn bank with Southerndown, where the layers of rock lie almost as regular as the layers in one of those tall, extra-special sponge cakes; nor are the sand dunes between Laugharne and Pendine anything like, not even in the remotest degree, the Pembrokeshire Stacks, where the seabirds breed in their thousands. And so it goes all the time: cockle gatherers scraping and riddling on the flats to the north of Gower; hard firm sand from Amroth to Saundersfoot; tearing currents between the rocky west Pembrokeshire cliffs and their islands; the cliffs and sandy beaches of Cardigan; cliffs guarding Cardiganshire's Lleyn; sandy beaches again almost from Llandudno to the Dee.

Taking a mile or so at a time, the list could be continued almost indefinitely. If I think of my coast as feminine then

Age cannot wither her, nor custom stale
Her infinite variety.

Changes take place, of course. Carmarthen Bay was once a forest, and I remember when I was a child going on to the Amroth shore after a vicious south-westerly storm, and all the lovely sands had gone and the fallen trees, dark-brown and peaty, lay everywhere; a tumble-down nightmare forest suddenly come out of the past, water desolate in pools between, and banks of slimy grey clay, on which the feet, booted or bare, slipped treacherously. I thought when I first saw that 'submerged forest' (as our elders and betters called it) that it was some new discovery, but I found out that its existence had been known for a long time, though it had never been seen quite so completely before. The same thing has happened on the shore of

Cardigan Bay, and in places also along the North Wales coast. In contrast there are places where the land creeps out to sea when river deposits and blown sand press the water back.

And sometimes there is the purely human change. I was talking to an old friend of a once familiar quiet beach that I had not visited for a few years.

"The worst of it was the difficulty of reaching it," I reflected. "And not a soul in sight to pull you out if you got stuck."

Dai stared at me. "How long since you been there, man? There's about a million caravans, tarred roads everywhere, not a square foot of sand to put your backside on, and enough noise from them little wirelesses you can't hear yourself think."

Change and decay, change and decay! Only, let's be fair, not always decay.

The complex mixture of geological causes that go to make up any few miles of coast is such a tangle that the boldest and most expert scientist might shrink from the task of trying to offer a simple explanation. There are so many kinds of rocks, hard and soft, old and new (give or take a few hundred million years), thick and thin, horizontal as a table, twisted by fire or volcanic action, sloping, tilting, vertical, undulating. The hard rock stays to become cliffs or mountains, the soft part erodes; the up and over curves are our cliffs, the down and under curves fill with sand and become beaches or sand-blown, marram-grass-held dunes. Only one thing remains, and that is the infinite variety—and, of course, the sea. Brought to the simplest terms, the earth's crust is made up of many layers; when the crust cooled it shrivelled like the skin of a baked apple. To me it is always something of a mystery, by which I mean I cannot, by any stretch of the imagination, relate it to myself or the time I live in. I stand in front of tortured rock layers going every-which-way, say beyond Saundersfoot, which I believe is a favourite homing ground for the illustrators of geology textbooks, and I can find no relationship in it whatever.

A primrose by a river's brim
A yellow primrose was to him
And it was nothing more.

Substitute 'strata' for Wordsworth's 'primrose', and you have something of the completeness of my mystification. I just cannot imagine a day when the sea, if sea there was, boiled and the cooling rocks heaved and seethed like porridge in a pot, and they twisted into those fantastic shapes.

Not that I complain. I have listened to the rebukes that were given to Job and, I hope, have profited from them:

> Where wast thou when I laid the foundations of the earth? declare, if thou hast understanding.
> Who hath laid the measures thereof, if thou knowest? or who hath stretched the line upon it?
> Whereupon are the foundations thereof fastened? or who laid the corner stone thereof?
> When the morning stars sang together, and all the sons of God shouted for joy?

The Levels of Monmouthshire end before Cardiff, and from the mouth of the Taff the harder rocks come swinging upwards to cliff height at Penarth Head and Lavernock Point. From now on it is up and down, cliffs falling to sandy beaches, promontories divided by burrows, where the sands blow in hard enough, as at Kenfig, to bury a city or fill a lake. The rivers bring down mud; in places the currents deposit it; some of the softer cliffs fall into the sea; some of the broken-down rocks are washed ashore again. Pebble banks are swept up; a change of current may clear a whole beach of its sand. Always change; seldom over short periods of time, though even that is not unknown, but, taking the long term view, stability is not the fashion of any coasts, except where they are fringed by the hardest rocks.

Even in the sea itself, the changes go on. In one place a sandbank shrinks, in another it grows. The Bristol Channel is one of the most dangerous coasts in this country, and it is a fair competitor even when compared with those of other countries. The list of shallows makes interesting reading reminiscent of the talk of old sailors: the Cardiff Grounds; the Old one-Fathom Bank; Nash, Middle Nash and West Nash Banks; Scarweather Sands; Outer Green Grounds; the Wolves; the Tusker; White Oyster Ledge. I have selected only a few at random. Is there a romantic sound to them? Forget that! They are not romantic at all. I'm not sure if there are less wrecks than when I was a boy, but then one-seventh of the total wrecks on the British coasts happened in the Bristol Channel. A Devonshire fisherman recited the couplet

> From Padstow Point to Hartland light
> Is a watery grave by day or night.

Llantwit Major Church
Gower coast

What he did not say (which was, maybe is, the truth) was that most of the Channel wrecks took place on the Welsh coast, though Cornwall and Devon, I admit, especially when most of the coastal craft were under sail, had a long sad list of their own.

Glamorganshire was once Morganwg, the land of Morgan. Its coastal plain, now pleasantly known as the Vale of Glamorgan, though there is not really a vale (Lowlands of Glamorgan would be more accurate), was always the main and the easiest way into the country. There was a narrow coastal strip on the north coast of Wales, but the mountains were higher and more inhospitable than the Glamorgan hills. There were a few passes, but not easy ones, in mid-Wales. So through the Vale has poured all the mixture of migrants—pre-history invaders, refugees, Romans, Normans—in search of good settlement land. And then, once more, when all invasions should have been at an end, came the Industrial Revolution, when the development of the coal and iron industries brought people flocking in again: from the Midlands; from Cornwall, which had miners but only a declining tin industry; from Scotland; from everywhere men lacked work; and we get the glorious amalgam that worked the Welsh valleys for a century. This constant flow of people, to and fro—for Wales sent out emigrants as well as it received them—has, in my opinion, led to misconceptions. The most common one is about the Flemings: that they settled in Gower and Pembrokeshire to such an extent that the people in those areas are not Welsh at all but practically English. To start with, if they had not been Welsh they would have been Flemish not English. But there is no true Flemish culture in South Wales; even the 'Flemish' chimneys of Pembrokeshire, we are assured now, are not Flemish at all. Where are the Flemish words that should have crept in? Where are the Flemish faces? No, anybody who has seen anything of the Flemings at home and noted their fervent racial prejudices would expect them to have lasted a bit longer and a little more obviously in an alien land. But they have not. The fact is that Wales always won in the end. Those who came fell into the melting pot and came out Welshmen.

Sabine Baring-Gould wrote in one of his books that Gower men would not marry Welsh women. With all due respect to the memory of Baring-Gould, Gower men chose their wives, the same as anybody else, for all sorts of reasons, but nationality is not and was not one of them.

Laugharne Castle

C

And again I have read more than once of the 'Englishry' and 'Welshery' of Pembrokeshire and how they never mixed. Well, I was brought up in the Englishry and went to school at Narberth in the Welshery, and I never in my life heard those labels except in a book. And we did mix, and, barring that the boys from the north could speak Welsh and the boys from the south as a rule could not, there was not a scrap of difference in us. We were all little Welsh boys (I hadn't realised I was a Saxon), and we were all equally horrid.

Out of the iron and coal industries three great ports grew. Cardiff was one, Barry the second, Swansea the third. Cardiff and Swansea always were towns of some importance; Barry in 1880 had seventeen houses and a population of about eighty. Now Barry has found a new prosperity in catering for holiday-makers, and whether the coaling ships come or do not come to the still fine docks cannot matter much. But the other two ports seesaw on the axis of industrial prosperity elsewhere, and only the expert economists can forsee what will happen to them in the future. The one thing I can guess is certain is that each has a future.

Cardiff has become the capital and one of the best laid-out capitals any country could wish to have. Whether it is as accessible to all parts as a capital should be is another matter. There are fine modern buildings, but the city has a long history and traditions going back far before the Romans, who built a castle on a British fortified site. What the Romans made was in turn built over by the Normans, who incorporated Roman work into their building. It has lasted well; a Roman wall is clearly in view still and looks as strong as it must have done when it was built.

A Duke of Normandy was a prisoner in Cardiff Castle for twenty-six years. He was Robert, brother of Henry I, and it was the king who kept him there. Mainly, the fortress was strong enough to prevent Welsh chieftains from giving trouble, but it was not strong enough to keep out Ifor Bach (Ivor the Little) who had been wronged by the Normans.

> At that time [wrote Giraldus] the Castle of Caerdyf was surrounded with high walls, guarded by one hundred and twenty men at arms, a numerous body of archers, and a strong watch. The city also contained many stipendiary soldiers; yet in defiance of all these precautions of security, Ivor, in the dead of night, secretly scaled the walls, and siezing the count and countess with their only son, carried them off into the woods, and did not release them until he had recovered everything that had been unjustly taken from him, and received a compensation of additional property.

Robin Hood could not have done better.

In 1404 Owain Glyndwr devastated both town and castle. One wonders *why* this man, far-seeing, liberal and progressive in so many ways, had this destructive streak in his nature that harmed friends as much as foes and probably was the cause of his being deserted in the end even by his own people.

Cardiff town has had further ups and downs too. Its martyr in Queen Mary's reign was an elderly fisherman, Rawlins White, as brave as he was obstinate, for he refused to escape when he had the chance to do so.

The place acquired a bad reputation for piracy, but it was a time when piracy (if you were not the victim) was a fairly respectable calling. Captain Henry Morgan came from Rumney, not far away. "Cardiff", said a magistrate, "is the general resort of pirates, where they are sheltered and protected." The trade must have lasted, for John Knight, King of Lundy, was the terror of the Channel between 1780 and 1790. The preventives said he was a smuggler, but his crew was between sixty and seventy and that is a pirate crew not an undercover smuggling gang. He went back to Lundy in the end, and I have never been able to find out what happened to him. Perhaps, like Morgan, he became a law-abiding, respectable citizen.

At the other, the western end, of the great curve of hard rocks the Severn currents have failed to wear away, is Swansea in the corner of Swansea Bay. Industry probably brought prosperity to Swansea, or to much of it, but from an aesthetic point of view it came near to ruining the ancient town of Sweyn's Ea, that was undoubtedly once a Scandinavian settlement. At one time there were 500 industries within a radius of twenty miles, and the devastation caused by chemical fumes was a hell Dante might have thought up. Yet there was, still is, another Swansea. "Genteel company and families are almost daily arriving in this gay resort of fashion . . . an assemblage of beauty and elegance fascinating beyond description."

That was more than 150 years ago, but, industry apart—and *that* is a lot less destructive than it was—the seaside town has something. Perhaps it is the sands, or the wide bay, or the hills from which the Tawe comes down from moorland as wild as any I have ever wandered on. Perhaps it is something of each of them. We all know cities which the factories and furnaces have made grim. Swansea is not grim. The new Civic Buildings are imposing, and the town centre is well planned, the gardens, especially, being a delight. But it would be unfair to look for antiquities in Swansea, for in the 1941 air raids it took about as bad a beating as any town could tolerate and still survive.

Industry still throws light shadows, and those from the chemical works float metaphorically across the sandy bay and the sparkle of the sea. But Swansea could become anything. Walter Savage Landor, who spent three years here at the end of the eighteenth century, thought the bay better than Naples: "Give me Swansea for scenery and climate". His first book of poems had just been published, and he was not yet the unhappy quarrelsome man he was to become. Swansea seems to have been the starting point for a number of literary figures whose lives ran into storms. Dylan Thomas was a Swansea man; Ann of Swansea, sister of John Kemble and Sarah Siddons lived here, made a sad marriage, died here, and now her books are forgotten.

And nearly forgotten also is T. J. Llewellyn Pritchard, who wrote a few books that won only local fame, though if you can get hold of his *Twm Shon Catti* it makes lively reading. Nobody could say it is a literary masterpiece, though Pritchard himself claimed it was the first Welsh novel. Half a century ago there was a copy, I should think, in half the farmhouse kitchens in South Wales. In many it may have been the only book besides the Bible. Some of it gives a lively picture of an earlier Wales. Leigh Hunt published a volume of Pritchard's poems in 1824, so he obviously had some talent, though at his worst he wrote the most awful lines:

Oh, list to the minstrel who sweeps the Welsh telyn [harp],
Hear, hear ye the harpings of Jeffery Llewelyn!

They say he had an artificial nose, a disfigurement that led to a lot of teasing from children "and the vulgar". He died about 1874 after a fall into the fire in front of which he had fallen asleep while reading.

I still say his *Twm Shon Catti* is fun to read.

Swansea has good libraries, museums, a university college and a first-rate art gallery. It is a centre already for culture in south-west Wales. It could become anything in the future . . . even "an assemblage of beauty and elegance fascinating beyond description". I am no prophet, the worst prophet in the world, but as an artistic centre it could outstrip Cardiff, leaving that city to the sad, solemn bowler-hatted civil servants.

I seem to hear the tinkle of a minuet from the Assembly Hall, where the 'genteel company' and families have gathered, and the ghost of Beau Nash (Swansea-born in 1674) nods over it all with an approving smile.

I have come too far west, though, for in the Vale of Glamorgan and around it there is much to visit, well within the reach of the sea winds that blow in the sand and bow the cliff trees until they grow as bent as ancient rheumaticky men.

Hardly five miles back is Neath, to which small ships once sailed easily. Neath, like Swansea was conquered by industry, but when it was a country town there was a fine castle which had probably been erected on a Roman foundation. There was also a beautiful Cistercian Abbey, and a description of it has come down to us:

> Like the sky of the Vale of Ebron is its covering; weighty is the lead that roofs this abode—the dark blue canopy of the dwellings of the godly. Every colour is seen in the crystal windows; every fair and high-wrought form beams through them like rays of the sun-portals of radiant guardians. Here are the gold-adorned choir, the nave, the gilded tabernacle work, on the glass, imperial arms; on the ceiling, kingly bearings; and on the surrounding border the shields of princes, the arms of Neath of a hundred ages.

All has gone. Only noble ruins now of what Leland said "semid to me the fairest abbay of al Wales".

If you are tired of the sound of the waves you can wander up the Vale of Neath and see some of the most picturesque waterfalls in the country. And so up to the high moorlands again, where curlews whistle mournfully over lonely standing stones that were put up thousands of years ago. Down at the river mouth is Briton Ferry, where you may safely cross, though in olden times it was a dangerous passage, as Giraldus discovered:

> We . . . proceeded along the sea-shore towards the river Neth, which on account of its quicksands, is the most dangerous and inaccessible river in South Wales. A packhorse belonging to the author, which had proceeded by the lower way near the sea, although in the midst of many others, was the only one which sunk into the abyss, but he was at last, with great difficulty, extricated, and not without some damage done to the baggage and books. Yet, although we had Morgan, the prince of the country, as our conductor, we did not reach the river without great peril, and some severe falls; for the alarm occasioned by this unusual kind of road, made us hasten our steps over the quicksands, in opposition to the advice of our guide, and fear quickened our pace; whereas, through these difficult passages, as we there learned, the mode of proceeding should be with moderate speed.

Eastwards again, and Port Talbot, on which the steel industry has laid its heavy hand. And, practically on the doorstep of the steelworks, another great church, Margam. Ruins now, but there is always some writer from the past to sing praises: "the noble Cistercian monastery of Margam" said Giraldus, "more celebrated for its charitable deeds than any other of that order in Wales". He told the story how one year the abbey corn ripened before its time because it was needed to feed the poor. "Their corn and provisions were perceptively, by divine assistance, increased, like the widow's cruse of oil by the means of the prophet Elijah."

Miracles were a commonplace at Margam Abbey: one young man who had siezed monastry lands went mad and died; another who started a fracas in the guests' hall was killed by an enemy and laid out on the very spot where he had caused the disturbance.

Now there are miracles no more; or perhaps they still happen and we lack the faith to see them. In our sophisticated age only babes and simpletons are aware of miracles.

Margam church now stands at the west end of the abbey, and there are only fragments of the earlier building. If the pattern is anything like that of the other dissolved monasteries, there must be much of its stone in every old house and barn for miles around. No countryside near a dissolved monastery looked far for dressed building stone in the sixteenth century. On Margam Mountain are relics of all the ages—earthworks, burial mounds, ancient camps—some of them looking out over the Channel.

Almost due south of Margam are the seaside delights of Porthcawl, but forgotten Kenfig and its lake Kenfig Pool come between. Porthcawl may be more fun, but Kenfig is more interesting. Who would believe that this was one of the important boroughs of Glamorgan, a walled town with a castle? There is so much to hear about Kenfig, and I confess I hardly know where history ends and legend begins. Or should it be the other way round? Under Kenfig Pool lies submerged an earlier city. Is that fact, I wonder, or some ancient folk memory? Was the sand blowing inland in pre-Norman times, perhaps in pre-Roman times? By the fourteenth century it was a flood at the gates, not as swift as Severn water, but equally persistent and destructive. When Leland came (early sixteenth century) what did he find? "There is a village on the Est side of Kenfik and a Castel, booth in ruines and almost shokid and devowrid with the Sandes that the Severn Se ther castith up."

By that time the burgesses could not balance their accounts "by reason of the overthrow, blowing and choaking up of sand in drowning of our town and church". From that one may guess that rents were not being paid. Nobody wants to pay rent for a sandhill.

At its most prosperous there were about 800 inhabitants. Ships came up the river. There was a council of burgesses and a portreeve, and the ordinances they drew up in Edward III's reign for the good rule of the town can still be studied—they might even be followed to advantage. Food had to be of good quality; tradesmen had to use the best materials. People must not throw rubbish into the streets; they had to pave opposite their own dwellings; animals were to pass through the streets "only going and coming to and from their pastures", and nobody was allowed to keep swine inside the town walls.

The paternal got very near the tyrannical at times: "Noe stranger shall walk by night after nine of the clock." Amusements were limited: "Noe manner of person shall play at dice, cards, bowles, nor no other unlawful games within the said town. . . . Brawlers and fighters that draweth blood the one upon the other shall pay three and fourpence for the bloodshed."

Even nagging wives were not forgotten: "It is ordained that if any woman be found guilty of scolding or railing . . . then she is to be brought at the first fault to the ducking stool there to sit one hour, and the second fault two hours and third fault to lett slippe [i.e. be ducked]."

It was a jury of six men who had to judge whether or not the scolds were guilty. I wonder who the men were. I can imagine many shaking their heads with the excuse, "I pray thee have me excused."

The last ordinance tells its own story: "Noe manner of person or persons whatsoever shall reap any sedges neither draw nor pull any rootes nor cutt any furzes in any place whatsoever, nor do any other thing that may be to the ruin destruction and overthrow of the said burrough."

Alas, neither grass roots nor good behaviour could hold back the flood that poured steadily on Kenfig. The waters of an inundation will subside, but the sand-flow knows no ebb.

From Kenfig it is a short distance to Porthcawl, and the way leads through Nottage, now pretty well lost in the popular resort. Ernest Rhys (I take him to be the Ernest Rhys who edited the Everyman Books) described Porthcawl a little over half a century ago:

Here is Porthcawl, a delightful little place for those who happen to like it.
The town is no more than a couple of streets or so, one ending in a paved,
wind-swept esplanade. Add to these a small dock and just as much shipping
of coal and limestone as may lend an air of business to a summer day, and
beguile the visitor into whiling away a lazy afternoon and thinking he has
done something, since a vessel has stowed her bunkers and put to sea: and
that is Porthcawl.

That *was* Porthcawl. The docks could not compete with those of
Barry and Cardiff, but somehow the visitors who happened to like
the place liked it better without coal and limestone, and the "delightful little place" has grown into a very big place, and the delights are
those the holiday-maker enjoys. In a way Barry has stepped out
along the same road. When I was a boy it was always Barry Dock,
or Barry Docks. Now it is Barry, the goal of a large percentage of
the holiday coaches in South Wales, and quite a few from the
Midlands and other places over the border as well. I do not know
which holiday resort is the more popular, but I suspect the Barry
people get a lot more profit from the holiday-makers than from the
docks.

The district, largely around Nottage, is the background for R. D.
Blackmore's *Maid of Sker*, which he wrote before he wrote *Lorna
Doone* (though its publication came later) and which some say is a
better novel. Sker House is still standing, or was recently—houses
go down and houses go up at such a rate these days that the author
has to be careful! The windswept cliff may be a housing estate or a
caravan park by the time this book gets into print. A sker, by the
way, is a ridge of rock running out to sea.

It is worth taking a short run inland from Barry to the villages of
Bonvilston and St. Nicholas, if only to see some of the best thatch-
work you can find in any part of the country. And from St. Nicholas
through a few lanes and across a few fields is an enormous cromlech
—about the most imposing one I have seen—known as the Tinkins-
wood Cromlech. I think somebody told me the stones go down to
the sea once a year to drink, but so many coastal cromlechs do that,
and it is difficult to remember which are the thirsty ones and which
are content to stay where they are.

Apart from the larger towns, the Vale is studded with interesting
and pretty villages, and many of them are on the coast or near it.
This was a famous settling ground for the Normans. They built
their castles and hoped their faults would be forgiven in return for
the churches they gave their money to. Architecture never was a

strong point in early Welsh art, and no doubt the ones the saints erected were meant more for praying in than for looking at. On these foundations the newcomers erected their arches, their piers of worked stone, their towers. If sometimes they went elsewhere to fight and conquer, here many of them hoped to be buried; here their effigies should mark their tombs.

In time they mingled and intermingled with the families of Welsh chieftains, and more than one romance concerns Norman knights and Welsh princesses, or Welsh lords and girls who spoke more Norman-Welsh than Anglo-Saxon. I'm not pretending to believe that all was harmony and peace in a very short space of time, but nobody in the Vale now claims to be Norman, while quite a few with Norman names claim part-Welsh descent.

There was a castle once at Lavernock, but this spot has a greater claim to fame in the fact that Marconi used it in his early transmitting experiments. He and George Kemp of Cardiff communicated with Flat Holm out in the Channel; and the Holms take us back into history again, for Flat Holm and Steep Holm were used as bases for Danish raids. There is a story that two of Thomas à Becket's murderers were imprisoned on Steep Holm, but for how long I never could find out.

Penmark, standing back from the coast, once had a castle belonging to the de Umfravilles. Aberthaw, a few miles away, was *nearly* a competitor in the struggle to become an important seaport. It does, though, have a slight claim to fame in that Smeaton used Aberthaw lime in the construction of his lighthouse on the Eddystone. St. Athan is noted as an Air Force Station, but I heard of St. Athan years before an Air Force was dreamed of.

And this was the way of it. Sir Laurence Berkerolles, Lord of St. Athan was blind, so he could not lead his followers when they went to hunt for Owain Glyndwr, who was reported to be in the neighbourhood. Two strangers came and begged hospitality, which the old man gave willingly. He apologised for the absence of so many of his household and explained the important work they were engaged on. In the morning as the visitors left one of them took the Anglo-Norman lord's hand in his. "Hand upon hand, heart upon heart," he said. "Owain Glyndwr thanks you for your hospitality and swears nothing will ever be done on his part to harm you or your house."

I heard another tale in a pub near here.

"You see that cottage back along the road a step?" said a man at the bar.

"The ruined one?"

"That's the one. Well, there was a old 'ooman, she was the last to live there. Her husband had been dead this thirty-forty year, Blodwen the Well they used to call her 'cause there's a well just by the cottage. She took bad and the minister went to see her, but she wouldn't be cheered up no way. 'My time is come,' she kep' saying. 'My time is come. I'll be in Adam's bosom any day now.'

" 'Abraham's bosom, you mean,' says the minister.

" 'What's the odds,' said Blodwen. 'Time anybody been a widow so long as me she don't care whose bosom it is'."

I thought I'd heard that one before, but I let it pass. The old chap was full of bits of stories and country expressions.

It was a chilly day. "Cold as a roadman's backside," he said. Later he repeated the expression.

"What's so cold about that?" I asked.

"You ever see a roadman?"

I had, of course.

"Well, there's only two ways you see a roadman. Either he's cleaning a gutter and then he's got his behind up in the air catching every wind that blows, or he's sitting sheltering from the rain in a hedge with his behind in the wet grass, and *that's* cold too. So there you are."

Actually the roadmen seem to be a vanishing race. It was a poor old job in bad weather, but it had its consolations. A good open-air life and passers-by to gossip to. The pay, I believe, was miserably low, but most of them ran a smallholding as a sideline. What should take their place to keep the country roadsides tidy was a problem for a few years, but recently a roadside trimmer that can cut verges or hedges seems to be in general use. It is a useful weapon; let us hope it will mean an end to that disastrous policy of poisoning the hedges with sprays that killed grass, shrubs—and everything else.

That, I'm sure no explanation is necessary, was madness.

The old roadmen of my youth usually seemed to have a bicycle, though I knew a few who had come from the pre-bicycle era, or from a time rather when a bicycle was an expensive luxury. The roadman trudging home in the dusk, or through the sunshine of a summer evening, was a familiar sight. The other popular libel on roadmen was that they were slow. Of some very unpopular man it would be said he ought to be chopped to pieces—"and put a roadman to do it".

Gray's ploughman could just as easily have been a roadman:

The ploughman homeward plods his weary way
And leaves the world to darkness and to me.

Neither the ploughman nor the infrequent roadmen plod any more. They go to work by car.

So many of the old ones were great characters. There was one up at Abergwessin, far enough from the coast, I'm afraid, but he really was an odd fellow. He always took off his coat when he had any hedging to do and worked in rolled-up shirt sleeves. His arms became a mass of scratches and cuts.

"Why don't you put your coat on while you're doing that?, Davy," they would ask. "Those thorns'll tear you to pieces."

He would contemplate his bleeding arms thoughtfully. "The Almighty will give me a new skin," was his reply. "But a good jacket costs money."

Gileston keeps alive the name of the Norman-English Giles family before they had descended to the yeoman status that the poet Blomfield gave his Farmer Giles. The tomb slab of Mary Giles (and Matthew) commemorates a woman who was murdered by a smuggler. You just can *not* get away from smugglers on this coast. But this one was French.

Llantwit Major is only a short trudge up from the shore, and it is one of the most interesting places on the Glamorgan coast. Its history goes so far back nobody can quite say when it started. The Ancient Welsh were here, then the Romans, and the legend is that the first Christian church was founded by Eurgain, a daughter of Caratacus. St. Paul is supposed to have preached here. Irish pirates destroyed the first church (I am writing legend and tradition as fact); and then St. Illtyd founded a monastic school in the sixth century. That, at least, is getting near fact, for Gildas the historian, Taliesin the poet, and St. David were all pupils. The monastery-university flourished until the Normans arrived, when it became a cell of Tewkesbury Abbey.

The church, one of the most interesting in the Vale, is a mixture of churches, and the building in use and ruins of earlier ones stand all together. There are inscribed stones and monuments of all dates from the eighth to the eighteenth century. There is a slab recording the death of Matthew Voss at the age of 129, and outside are the remains of a dovecot, a gatehouse and a tithe barn.

There is a fifteenth-century town hall, above which hangs a pre-Reformation bell. The 'Old Swan' was a mint, and—need I say it—a haunt of smugglers. Fourteenth century Ty-mawr, also was used by them.

St. Donat's is best known at present as the headquarters of the Atlantic College, but I know hardly anything about that except that it seems to turn out a breed of near-supermen; also that it is international and young men come to it from all parts of the world.

But St. Donat's is an ancient village and has an ancient history. The great focal point was the castle (now the college), and they say that it has never been uninhabited, though it must have been in poor shape after the Civil War, and by 1800 a farmer, the curate and the village schoolmaster shared it. The family most associated with it were the Stradlings, but Randolph Hearst, the American newspaper proprietor, was the man who spent money on it and restored it to its former glory. There is a fine church containing Norman work here, and in it are the tombs of many Stradlings. The fifteenth-century tower, so the story goes, was built by Sir Henry Stradling in order to watch out for a Breton pirate who had once held him to ransom. He caught him, too. You'd think at least he'd have returned the compliment and got his high ransom back, but no, after the pleasant manner of the times, he had him buried in the sands up to his neck and left him to the tide.

Dunraven also has its castle, dating from only the nineteenth century, though on a site that had had a Norman one on it (and that, as likely as not, on a British one). It belonged first to the de Londres family, which was Norman, who gave it to the Butlers, from whom it was acquired by the Carmarthenshire Vaughans. They are said to have been pirates. Perhaps they were; as I said earlier, it was a respectable profession in the sixteenth century, though I cannot quite see where they had a harbour big enough to hold a ship of any size.

Ogmore Castle stands a little way back from the sea. Crossing the river near it are picturesque stepping-stones, and the combination of these and the ruined castle is irresistible to photographers, and it is said that this is the most photographed spot in Glamorganshire. It is very old, about twelfth-century at least, but there is not much history related of it. Like St. Donat's, it belonged to the de Londres, and quite early a William de Londres married a Welsh girl, and that may have saved it from Welsh attacks.

From Ogmore the Tusker Rock can be seen a few miles out to sea. This was one of the most notorious danger spots in bad weather for shipping, and it has been the cause of many wrecks.

Out of all the stories of smuggling, wrecking and piracy that are told of so many spots on this coast, one fact must be borne in mind, and I know it is true for I lived a very long time on Carmarthen Bay. Whenever there was a wreck in which a vessel was broken up, a lot of stuff—both timber and cargo—was washed ashore. Local people, especially the unemployed and the unemployable, were on the look-out always for this flotsam, and some made a very good thing out of it. Collecting wreck was known as wrecking. So perhaps some of the 'wreckers' were not the wholly wicked men they have been thought to be. I shall have more to say on this subject when I am on the shores I have actually lived on.

So back to Swansea, and on to a unique piece of the Glamorganshire coast, the peninsula of Gower. The influence of settlers and invasions I have mentioned earlier. The people who have settled in Gower through the ages have, naturally, influenced it and left their mark. But I am sure it remained Welsh and still is Welsh, with a marked similarity to Carmarthenshire rather than Glamorgan, if a comparison is needed, just as the Cardiganshire type of Welshman trails down into north-Pembrokeshire Precellies. Some early writers made too much of this anglicising business. Baring-Gould for instance said that since the Conquest "Gower has been English in population." The fact is that hardly any two districts in Wales are alike in physical character or in the characteristics of the people. Caernarvonshire people are in many ways very different from those of equally Welsh Cardiganshire. Radnor people are not like those who live in the mining valleys; Pembrokeshire men are quite dissimilar from the inhabitants of Flint. But, taking into account immigrations and new blood, the stock is the same.

I would not dwell on this point so much or so persistently were it not that I feel that this insistence on differences does nobody any good service. There have always been too many divisions in Wales; it was for long a number of very small princedoms. Even yet the North Walian says the South Walian cannot speak correct Welsh. This niggling at each other does not help anybody. Giraldus, centuries ago, recognised what disservice division did to the nation:

If their princes were unaminous and inseparable in their defence; or rather, if they had only one prince, and that a good one; this nation, situated in so powerful, strong and inaccessible a country, could hardly ever be completely overcome. If, therefore they would be inseparable, they would become insuperable.

Good advice but it was never heeded.

But everyone is for division nowadays. Cornwall, they tell me, is on the brink of setting up home rule; while Yorkshire (from which I believe some of my hotch-potch of ancestors came, though there is a suspicion that there was a Scotsman or two among them) has already chosen its future Prime Minister.

But me, I follow the Psalmist: "Behold, how good and joyful a thing it is, brethren, to dwell together in unity." The day the Nationalists throw me out as a superfluous Saxon I shall go straight to London and whitewash on every milkman's and draper's window: *Welshmen, Go Home!* So look you out Morgan the Milk, and Dickens and Jones, Oxford Street, the Cloth; when your compatriots reject me I'm on my way.

The greater part of the Gower coast is a series of cliffs alternating with wide sandy bays. The north coast is on the Loughor Estuary and tends to be more flat. It is marshy in places, and there is plenty of sand, but there are some uninviting mud-flats as well.

From Swansea there is the wide curve of Swansea Bay sweeping out to Mumbles Head. Mumbles, now mainly a holiday resort, is a delightful little town, even though

> Mumbles is a funny place,
> A church without a steeple;
> Houses built of old ships wrecked
> And a very peculiar people.

After Mumbles there are miles of small bays and one large one, Oxwich Bay. Dividing them are the cliffs and the capes. The best-known bays are Langland Bay, Caswell Bay, Brandy Cove (smuggling rears its ugly head again!), the broad length of Oxwich, Port Eynon Bay; then a long stretch, mainly cliffs, out to the noble promontory called Worm's Head that is visible from almost anywhere on Carmarthen Bay. A good barometer it was too from the far side. Seen sharp and clear it generally meant rain, though the waggish natives of South Pembrokeshire used to say if you could see Worm's Head clearly it was going to rain, and if you couldn't see it, it *was* raining. The same simple joke served also for Lundy Island.

After Worm's Head the shore flattens out into sandy beaches for the most part. Nowadays most of the area is ideal holiday country, but in the days before everybody made for a fortnight by the sea as a matter of course, I believe it was a coast to be avoided by shipping. In bad weather there have been some notable wrecks. The most unusual happened in January 1868 and involved sixteen ships. There was not even a storm, though there were, it is said (naturally most of the details have come down by mouth), a nasty ground swell and some breakers. Altogether eighteen or nineteen boats, from 80 to 400 tons, were outward bound. One or two managed to clear the point called Burry Holms, the next northerly cape to Worm's Head. The wind dropped, the tide was on the flood (coming in), and the sixteen unfortunate boats drifted up Broughton Bay. It seems to have turned into a shambles. A couple of them were driven on some rocks, others collided, but for the most part they just had their keels smashed in by bumping on the shallows in the heavy swell. A few men were rescued by the pilot boat which stood by all night. Because it *was* night, nobody in the bay knew what was happening, so there was no attempt at rescue. When morning came the sixteen ships were in pieces. From Burry Holms the five miles or so to Whitford Point was strewn with "broken spars, hulls of vessels, ropes and large strewage of coal". Also, as might be expected, drowned sailors. The sailors were buried in a number of the neighbouring church-yards.

A ghost story was told of that awful night. A choirboy going to choir practice in Llanmadoc Church was scared into a faint as he crossed the churchyard. When he recovered, he said he had seen "a man looking through the church window". Everybody said he had seen the ghost of one of the drowned sailors. Taking Llanmadoc as being roughly a mile from the shore it was surely more likely that one who had got ashore alive had managed to reach the church.

It seems incredible that sixteen experienced sea captains who knew the coast (and they had a pilot cutter) should have been caught in the same way. But about this catastrophe there is much that is incredible.

Inland, Gower is moderately hilly, and I have been told that the soil is poor. But the climate is so pleasant that you do not notice much barrenness, and in the valleys everything seems to flourish and flower with abandon. There are many ruins of old castles—the finest being Oystermouth near Mumbles—and at least one fine cromlech, Arthur's Stone above Reynoldstone. Another thirsty stone, for once a year it comes down to the sea to drink. This is, from all points of view, an unsatisfactory exercise, because catastrophe would strike any person who saw it happen.

The churches are for the most part small and sturdy. Several have saddle-back roofs, a characteristic of churches in this neighbourhood.

The coast is noted for its limestone caves. A few are well-known, but in truth parts of the peninsula are riddled with them. Many have evidently been inhabited in prehistoric times and there is much evidence of that in the bones and so on that have been discovered. The most famous is the Red Lady found in Paviland caves near Rhossili. The redness apparently is iron oxide, and 'she' was no lady; she was a man. I think modern cave men feel they have still a lot to discover in the peninsula.

The coast of Gower, on its more popular beaches, is becoming a playground, but the delights of the big resorts are absent, so it is, if one may put it, a pleasant, quiet playground. Nowhere in the district are you far from the sea, and once away from the caravans, the tents, the boarding houses there are quiet lanes, breezy hill-tops, moors and quiet unspoiled villages.

The north is less popular with holiday makers, perhaps because the sands of the estuary are a bit too wide. Yet up here is one of Gower's most individual villages. It is Pen-clawdd and (though cockles are found and harvested elsewhere) the real queen of Cockle Villages. I say queen because so many of the cockle gatherers are women, as indeed they always have been. The sands at low tide are wide, miles wide they seem to the stranger. The cockle-gatherers go out with their donkey carts and pony carts; they rake up the cockles, riddle them, put the cockles into the carts, and when the tide turns return with their harvest. Nobody can describe adequately this way of life. It is fascinating. It is not romantic—one dear woman told me in a few sentences well decorated with adjectives (mainly *that* one) that it was hard work for small money—but it is an ancient craft. The twentieth century should have seen it out, but I think it will be the other way round. The cockle gatherers have strong personalities, express their opinions freely, are very independent, but are as kind and hospitable as Giraldus said all Welshmen were, "they consider liberality and hospitality amongst the first virtues".

Marros Church
The coast trees lean away from the wind

A few years ago, so I was told, there was an old cockle-gatherer known as Dai-cocos-bach, which presumably translates into Little Dai Cockles. He had a donkey and cart, and he divided his time between gathering cockles and the bar of the local pub. One night some of the local lads unharnessed his donkey and let it go. Some time after the pub closed Dai came out and went to where he had left his donkey and cart. He stood staring at the cart and scratching his head.

"Well!" he exclaimed at last. "If I'm Dai Cocos I ha' lost a donkey, but if I be somebody else I've found a cart.

There are only a few villages that, like Pen-clawdd, still live on an old peasant industry. We cannot afford to do without one of them.

The cliffs of South Pembrokeshire

D

# CHAPTER 3

# PONTARDULAIS TO AMROTH

THE south-eastern corner of Carmarthenshire, which is the part north of Gower, has for long been a centre of industry, and whatever its virtues may be, prettiness is not one of them.

From Pontardulais down to Loughor, across to Llanelly, or Llanelli as they spell it now (quite correctly for it was the llan of St. Elli), on to Burry Port and, completing the triangle, back to Pontardulais again, there has been a concentration of those occupations that create wealth rather then beauty. I know that coming down from Ammanford the best time was the evening when the lights from the various factories sparkled all over the valley like fallen stars: to make it more interesting they were, where chemicals were the stock in trade, stars of many colours. And I must have been very young indeed when, on clear evenings, people would point across the whole bay from its western curves to show you the lights of Burry Port and the glow of the works to the east of it.

Well, many mines have closed, and the fortunes of other industries fluctuate; some are going from the scene and some have gone for ever. What exactly lies in the future it is hard to foretell. The idea behind most planning seems to be that the thing to do is bring in light industries where heavy ones fail. This may work. It is to be hoped something will be done to keep people employed. Too many remember with bitterness the 1930s, when men could go unused for decades; a repetition of that hardly bears thinking of. The one thing that can be said is that a social conscience has developed and that authority does *try* to help where once it shook its head and said how sad it all was.

I think, after Burry Port and Pembrey, we can, moving westward, be considered back in the country again. But the beaches are hardly among the best Wales has to offer. All the rivers flowing into the Burry and Loughor estuaries have brought quite a lot of good Carmarthenshire soil down with them. More comes down the Gwendraeth past Kidwelly. Then the Towy does its share. Add the eastward drift of sand in the prevalent south-westerlies and a few helpful currents, and you get as fine a stretch of sandbanks, shallows and sandy burrows as can be found anywhere along the coast. Even the railway from Pembrey up to Kidwelly keeps well back from the sea, though after Kidwelly it runs close to the east Towy bank. I have been told that this coast is almost unnavigable for ships of any size; pleasure-boating, unless you know where you are going, is chancy; and, though my practical experience here is nil (I know the black look of it well enough), it is not any good for picnics or for swimming.

Where the Towy estuary enters the sea there are vast flat expanses of mud and sand at low tide, choppy shallow water when the tide comes in. On the west are Laugharne sands, more cockle grounds and a sandy waste called East Marsh. On the east are Cefn Sidan sands. A little way up river are Llanstephan on the west, Ferryside on the east. I suppose there must have been a ferry at some time, perhaps there still is, though to get from one bank to the other all I have ever done (apart from the many occasions I was in a train) has been to go up to Carmarthen by some very tortuous lanes and back down to Llanstephan by wider but only slightly less twisty ones.

Once large ships went up as far as the quays of Carmarthen town, but in those days a 'large' boat was what we would consider a very small one now. The channel changes and has always been subject to change; expert knowledge was needed to pilot anything bigger than a local coracle safely into the Towy. The cockle gatherers know their way over the wide stretches: strangers do well to be wary. Ships have been wrecked; it is easier to get into the shallows than to get out of them. Even three whales once found their way into the bay and were beached there.

This area, where the Towy and the other rivers, two Gwendraiths and Taf, reach the sea, has submerged over the centuries, or been covered by sandbanks, for beyond Cefn Sidan sands the lost village of Halkin lies beneath the waves.

There is no easy way along this coast. The railway followed it as much as it could, presumably because the industries of the Swansea area and south Carmarthenshire lay near it, but the flats of Ferryside must have been the last straw, and the trains turned right and went upriver to Carmarthen, and the railway stayed inland until it reached Tenby. Mind, on a fine sunny day the estuary between Ferryside and Llanstephan can look delightful as the light breezes ripple the water. On a cold grey misty day it can look equally dismal and un-inviting. From, say, Burry Port to Pendine, which marks the end of the sands and sand dunes that start at Laugharne, is no great step by sea. To get from one to the other by the coastal lanes could take half a day, or if, like I do, you get lost now and then, you could even take a day on the journey.

From Llanstephan village you can go down to the shore round the castle. There across the water of the Taf is Laugharne, hardly more than a stone's throw: a small stone and a very strong thrower! The last time I went from Llanstephan to Laugharne I turned right in the former village and took the country lanes. Very quiet they were on that summer day, and a good thing they were for they were so narrow I might have been a very large train in a very small tunnel, and there were neither passing places nor lay-bys. The lanes went up hills and down hills, and from the tops the estuary often came into sight. There were tiny hamlets and one small village, Llanybri; a chapel, some farms, cottages, and fields full of either very good crops or very good milking cows. The whole area (as is much of South Carmarthenshire) is a complete criss-cross of small lanes, few of which are used by more than one or two farms. After a long, long drive (or so it seemed), we were out on the main Carmarthen road a few miles from St. Clears. To get to Laugharne we turned left, and six or seven miles on ordinary winding country road brought us to Laugharne. It was a long way to have come to cover that metaphorical stone's throw across the Taf.

From Laugharne it is easy. Coast road behind the sand dunes to Pendine, then cliff road, with dips into wide bays at Amroth and Saundersfoot, all the way to Tenby—and beyond it.

After the industrial area to the west of Swansea we are back in real country again at Kidwelly, which should be spelt Cydweli. At one time it was a notable little seaport, but the coastal trade of the small ships is a memory of the past. The castle, though, is a fine ruin. It ranked in size with Pembroke and Caerphilly, and its early history was stormy from the twelfth century, when it was built by a Bishop of Salisbury, until the Civil War, when men realised at last that strong stone walls were no longer a refuge from their enemies.

The most famous incident in the history of this castle was the attack on it made by a Welsh army that was led by a woman, Gwenllian, wife of Gruffydd ap Rees. While he kept the Normans

busy in North Wales, she brought an army to attend to those in the
south. Her army was defeated by Marice de Londres, and Gwenllian
and one of her sons were killed. There are conflicting accounts of
what did happen, but the best-known is that they were captured and
executed on the battlefield. This incident caused great bitterness.
There was no Welsh Bible then, so perhaps they did not know "All
they that take the sword shall perish with the sword", but even as
late as this century they would write: "Long indeed did the Normans
of our land rue the stroke that beheaded Gwenllian. Blood ran like
water and steel flashed like lightning to avenge the foul murder."

A few years after the battle at Kidwelly the Normans were
defeated at Cardigan. A wooden bridge over the river collapsed, and
thousands of Normans were drowned in the Teifi. I would not have
supposed any bridge there would hold "thousands" but enormous
numbers of prisoners were taken—by women some accounts say—
and, customs being what they were and feelings running high, there
can be little doubt that the Welsh heroine's death was suitably
revenged.

Between Kidwelly and Carmarthen there is one good road;
between the road and the Towy is the usual maze of lanes, used
mainly by farmers. The one thing you can say of these parts is that,
if you are not in a hurry and do not mind being lost for a while,
you could not choose a pleasanter land to be lost in. And a point
worth keeping in mind is that what Giraldus wrote centuries ago
still holds good: "they consider liberality and hospitality among the
first virtues".

I cannot promise that kindness now goes quite as far as it did
then. He described how everybody, household and visitors, all slept
together at night on the floor of the main chamber. "The fire con-
continues to burn by night as well as by day, at their feet, and they
receive much comfort from the natural heat of the persons lying
near them." Shades of Chaucer and *The Reeve's Tale*!

He admitted the floor felt rather hard when you had been lying
on it for a while.

Between Kidwelly and Ferryside is the little hamlet of St.
Ishmael's. This was once connected with the drowned village of
Halkin, but it is difficult to make out exactly what that connection
was, since Halkin itself is only a memory. I have a drawing of a
chair that once stood in St. Ishmael's Church. It had two seats with
an arm between, rather like a small settee with an arm. The date

was 1655, and the initials, R.M., were probably those of the maker. Two texts were carved one above the other: "Husbands love your wives" and "Let the wife reverence her hus".

In this chair in olden days quarrelsome couples were made to sit during service. There is no evidence as to whether these penances worked (there is no reason why they should not), but the congregations must have enjoyed it very much.

As one old chap said to me, "You had to make your own amusements in them quiet times".

I am sorry to say the chair has quite disappeared; it may have been thrown out during the nineteenth-century restoration, though it is not impossible that it still lies in some old farmhouse attic. Or, of course, the married couples of St. Ishmael's may have given up quarrelling.

Ferryside must have been some sort of a hamlet since there was a ferry. Llanstephan is more popular, but Ferryside has not lacked its admirers.

> Like Llanstephan, it has been endowed with every feature this earth has to give—sea, river, bay, sands, headlands, green swelling hills with all their variety of form, planting their feet on the waters. From the hill-top appear the mountains, the Glamorganshire coast, sweet Rhossili Bay, Worm's Head with its curious form, its solitariness, its wild grand scenery, its historic interest; and you think of the Roman sentinel, who once kept watch on its lonely shore.

That is an extract from a book privately printed by Clay, London, in 1880. The author was Mary Curtis, about whom nothing seems to be known, and it is called *The Antiquities of Laugharne, Pendine and Their Neighbourhood* (and covers a lot more). It is something of a curiosity, running to 339 pages of small print and describing the countryside from Laugharne to Begelly in Pembrokeshire, where the gypsies still, as they have always done, live on the moor. It contains a lot of interesting gossip and is useful as a guide book, even today.

The Roman sentinel was a romantic touch, and I fail to see why he should have kept watch over Ferryside, but the Romans did get as far as Carmarthen (Maridunum), and further north in the county they mined gold in the hills.

Carmarthen was Merlin's town. His oak, the very, very little left of it, stands in a road junction on the road out to Abergwili, and the prophecy is

When the oak falls down
Then sink shall the town.

Carmarthen people have taken every possible precaution against
disaster, with iron railings and cement buttressing, but, my word,
the old creature does look decrepit at times. Still we all hope it
stands for a long, long while yet.

Sir Richard Steele's second wife 'Dear Prue' was a member of the
local Scurlock family; and he lived in Carmarthen for the last few
years of his life, died there and was buried there, though Prue was
buried in Westminster Abbey. Theirs was a strange, in some ways
a touching story. She could be contrary at times, "pretty, peevish
Prue—spoilt-child, wilful and shrewd, contrary and charming
woman".

But behind the disputes there must have been deep affection. "I
love you better than the light of my eyes or the life-blood of my
heart", he wrote; while there is among some manuscripts in the
British Museum a piece of paper on which she had written

Ah, Dick Steele, that I were sure
Your love, like mine, would still endure;
That time, nor absence, which destroys
The cares of lovers, and their joys,
May never rob me of that part
Which you have given of your heart;
Others unenjoy'd may possess
Whatever they think happiness.
Grant this, O God, my great request:
In his dear arms may I for ever rest.

Ernest Rhys, writing about 1910 of the days of his boyhood, some
of them spent at Carmarthen, remembered, "At the quay usually lay
two or three of the coasting vessels that brought coal and timber to
the town moored below the bridge". Well the days when the town
could consider itself a seaport are far back in the past, though, with
the farmers from one of the most fertile pasture valleys flocking into
town, it looks more prosperous now than it can have done then.
Prices have risen a little since John Taylor, the water poet (1580-
1653) visited Carmarthenshire and praised its fine food and low
prices.

Butter, as good as the world affords, 2½d or 3d the pound; a salmon two foot
and a halfe long, twelve pence. Biefe, 1½d a pound; oysters 1d the 100: egs,
12 or a penny. A little money will buy much, for there is nothing scarce
dear or hard to come by but tobacco pipes.

Llanstephan lies across the Towy estuary opposite Ferryside. The village has grown quite a lot since I first knew it, but it is still well off the main road, for, excepting the maze of lanes I mentioned earlier, it is really the end of the road. There is no bridge across the Towy to Ferryside, nor one to Laugharne across the Taf. I suppose, with a good little rowing boat *and* an equally good knowledge of the tides and the sandbanks, you could visit the three in less than an hour. To visit them by the minor roads could, unless you knew every un-signposted little lane, mean a long journey. Using the main roads and going up to Carmarthen between each might cut a day's travelling down to a half-day or less. It depends on how fast you go and how often you stop. Not that the main road is tempting— in the traffic procession you can't stop—but off the Carmarthen - Tenby road there are many places where the scenery is worth more than a glance.

Quiet Llanstephan is dominated on the seaward side by the hill-top ruins of the castle the de Clares built in the twelfth century. There is a healing well, St. Anthony's well, near it; what it cured I never could find out, though as a rule a good healing well was a help in all ills. People who used it, and a lot did in an age when faith was stronger and doctors were rare, had to drop in a pin as payment.

As for Laugharne, this is a very ancient village town, with a charter that dates back to 1307 and a portreeve and burgesses to govern it. It is quiet and unspoiled, clean and cheerful and bright, and its ivy-covered castle looks out across a wide foreshore to what I suppose are the cockle grounds. To the best of my knowledge these are the most westerly of them, or the most productive in the west. Actually you can pick up your cockles at low tide almost anywhere there is sand in the miles between here and Saundersfoot, but I don't think they are worth going for in a big way. In the spring tides many people knew where to find mussels, but these made some of them ill. When I was a boy our cockle-man came from Laugharne with a small pony-cart. He must have travelled many miles. The cart was full of cockles, and when he came near a house or village he let out a blood-curdling yell that I suppose translated into "Fresh Cockles!" Most people liked them, and most people bought them. A few pennyworth made a saucepanful, and there, with fresh bread and butter, was a teatime delicacy. Everyday delicacies were not so common then, and the cockle-man was always sure of a welcome. I never knew his name but I can remember his face. I hope he made a good thing out of his wares, for, if only in the miles he trudged (I suppose he *could* ride, gipsy-fashion, on the shaft of his cart), he worked hard for what he got.

At one time some of our schoolchildren thought out the jolly game (easy pleasures were not much more common than easy tea-time treats) of hiding behind hedges and lobbing large, turfy clods into the cockle-man's cart. My father, who was the village school-master dealt with this game swiftly and effectively, and the amusement lost its attractions and was not repeated.

My daddy was, as the expression goes, "a beast, but a just beast!"

A man severe he was, and stern to view
.    .    .    .    .
Full well the busy whisper, circling round,
Convey'd the dismal tidings when he frown'd;
Yet he was kind.

Many an offence that now might end in a juvenile court he cured as he went along. Parents did not question his justice, and I don't think, in forty years, the naughtiest pupil bore malice.

The great magician Merlin made a prophecy: "Kidwelly was, Caermarthen is, and Laugharne will be, The greatest city of the three". Well, it is the business of magicians to make prophecies, and as a rule we are charitable enough to forget the ones that don't come true. But Kidwelly *was* long ago probably much more important than Carmarthen; to think of Laugharne as busier than Carmarthen is on its market days does seem rather a silly idea, but when you come to think of it Laugharne has something that Carmarthen has not. It has a famous poet. I am no critic and I do not know whether Dylan Thomas had a great talent or a small spark of genius —or even a large spark of genius—but the host of his admirers grows, and, among Americans in particular, admiration is sometimes toppling over into reverence. While this book was being written, his house, the Boat House, was saved from demolition. If the Dylan cult grows, Carmarthen could yet have its nose put out of joint— and the prophecy would come true.

Between Laugharne and the sea is a sandy waste called East Marsh which stretches as far as Pendine. Between East Marsh and the sea is a fine stretch of sand, also going as far as Pendine. The Ordnance Survey Map calls them Laugharne Sands, but I never heard them called anything but Pendine Sands. They are firm and hard at the Pendine end, but I have come across some very soft patches nearer Laugharne. Usually they were quiet and near-deserted (it seems incredible when you see the traffic and people on them today), and young men with cars could have great fun driving their cars up and down, flat-out. But there was a belief that about five miles up from Pendine the sand became soft and you *could* get stuck. So as a rule we did not go too far. My own first motor was a smart little BSA three-wheeler, and at Pendine I got it up to the (then) incredible speed of sixty miles an hour! That really was going some! But one day I noticed my wheel tracks were looking rather deeper—and deeper . . . so I turned hurriedly and made for Pendine. I did know a man once who actually had to leave his little Rover flat-twin as the tide came in and get it hauled away when the tide went out, but that was close to the village and west of it.

On high days and bank holidays motor-cycle races were held on Pendine sands, and great fun they were. I was at an age then to enjoy noisy exhausts and the smell of racing oil.

More serious were the attempts on car speed records. Malcolm Campbell was often in Pendine and so was Parry Thomas. Campbell was, this was the general impression, a bit proud and stand-offish, but Parry Thomas was matey, and everybody thought the world of him. Then came that awful day when the driving chain of his car snapped and killed him. I don't know what happened after that, but the zest for record-breaking on Pendine sands dwindled away. They buried Babs, Parry Thomas's car, among the sand dunes.

While I was writing this book a suggestion was made that Babs should be dug up, restored, and put in a museum. The reaction in Pendine was swift and as fierce as it was unexpected. Different people expressed themselves in different ways, but the sum of it was expressed in the phrase: *Over my dead body*! So, presumably, Babs will stay where they put it and where Parry Thomas himself apparently wished it to be if anything went wrong.*

Behind the sand dunes the road runs from Laugharne much as it always did, but Pendine itself has, on the eastern fringe, altered beyond recognition. There is some sort of weapon-testing station here; it may be top secret, I wouldn't know. I don't go much for weapons any more—I've reached the sword-into-ploughshare stage of life. The tiny horse-and-gambo, church-outing village of my childhood seems at first glance to have vanished, and what has taken its place is almost a little town. Yet, curiously, at the western end,

* They have changed their minds. It *is* being dug up.

where the road climbs up to the hill that runs like a backcloth most of the way from Laugharne, I see the same inns, the same old houses—and the gradient of the steep hill is the same too! The same farms by the roadside, the same old church, the same old inn at Green Bridge, and the same road leading to the same quiet, deserted Marros.

It is rather strange about Pendine church. It is on the top of a steep hill, and it must be about a mile from the village it is named after and which it serves. I was thinking about this one day, when the penny dropped. So are nearly all the coastal village churches. Marros church is about a mile from the sea (no village there, though). Amroth church is, too, and St. Issell's at Saundersfoot, and many, many more. Suddenly I can hardly think of a Welsh coast church that stands right by the sea. In Cardigan Bay there are a few. At Cwm-ar-Eglwys in north Pembrokeshire they built it almost on the beach, but the sea took most if it away in a storm, and there is only a bit of churchyard left. There is a church close against the sea at Llangelenin in Merionethshire and one so close at Llanaber further up the coast that on a stormy night it would be the noise of pounding waves rather than coughing that "drowns the parson's saw". But generally you can reckon on a mile between sea and church. Now this *could* mean nothing at all, but I think it means that the churches were erected near fortified spots where people could take their goods and animals when raiders or pirates paid a visit. And if the churches were, in their young days, used for the same purpose it would account for the fact that so many churches, especially the towers, look like miniature fortresses.

There are two ways of going on foot from Pendine to Amroth. If you know the tides and the shore it is very easy to walk all the way along the sands (though it includes some rocky scrambling). If you are completely familiar with the coast you can, in fact, get nearly all the way to Tenby, and in the few places where the tide never gets out quite far enough there are good cliff paths. There are cliff paths over all the little capes, but they are not always easy to find. A few go very near the cliffs and are not safe everywhere. But if it is scenery you want then they are magnificent.

The main road goes a mile or so back from the sea. A bungalow has sprung up here and there, but on the whole this road has not changed much in half a century and I could swear that the same wind-pleached trees are still there, leaning over the road as if pushed down by the south-westerlies that come roaring over, especially in autumn and spring.

Marros is the only 'place' on the road, and it does not even seem to be a hamlet. That, of course, is deceptive for there are a number of farms and cottages in the area, though I do not think there is a post office, and the nearest inn is at Green Bridge. The church stands out, strong and sturdy—and very lonely in its group of wind-swept trees. The hill is called Marros Mountain—never was such a miniature mountain—and the level bit of road Marros Plain. Many, many years ago somebody told me a battle was fought on Marros Plain. That could have been a folk memory of some skirmish be-tween a raiding party and the local people. Being then at an age when battles were romantic, I could hear in the wind the clash of sword on armour and the war cries of brave knights.

So all day long the noise of battle roll'd
Among the mountains by the winter sea.

It did not need much to set my imagination on fire in those days.

"He reads too many books", said the neighbours.

"Always got his nose in a book", said another.

Our butcher was more blunt. "No good ever come of reading them old books. Won't come to no good that boy, you'll see."

I have heard a legend that the natives used to take refuge in the church from wolves. Substitute a few sea-raiders for 'wolves' and the thing fits together.

These traditions of battles long ago are often heard in remote places. There had been one fought, I was told, on Crunwere Mount-ain (which again is no mountain, only a rounded hill top), and that can be only a few miles inland from Marros. I took that so seriously that I persuaded a friend to come and see if we could find any evidence of it. I think I expected rusty armour and broken swords. but there was only the breast-high bracken and the wind in our faces and the pipits clicking in front of us. Much better really! Down in the valley was Garner's Mill. I don't think it was working but it was still complete. When I got to reading The Mill on the Floss it was Garner's Mill I saw, and I saw it again in Hardy's The Trumpet Major.

Quiet though it appears, Marros had an annual fair until the mid-nineteenth century. It was held on 21st August, and always the local farmers brewed beer for Marros Fair—and sold it. Local publicans (there were pubs at Pendine and Amroth) did not like this as it interfered with their trade, so they managed to get the brewing forbidden. I have heard that police were sent into the district to enforce the new rule. The local home-brewers took their revenge by upsetting a few bee-hives in a field near where the fair was being held, and the bees, understandably feeling rather peeved, chased the lot of them, merrymakers, police and legitimate publicans, and it ended in everybody running home. The fair was never held again.

From Pendine the walk over the sands is, or was when I walked it—which I have done dozens of times—easy but you had to be crafty; though, even if you mistimed the tides, there was only one danger spot. Close to the village was a small point called Dolwen Point. Beyond was a fair promentory, all rocky. That was (is) Ragwin Point. Beyond Ragwin was a wide clean sweep of bay to Telpin Point, then another smaller sweep to Black Rocks, and at Black Rocks was the stream that divided Carmarthenshire from Pembrokeshire.

If you left Pendine just in time to get clear round Dolwen you could get over Ragwin by scrambling over the rocks the tide had cleared. If you were smart you got practically round Telpin at low tide, and that made Black Rocks easy to clear as it was a very small cape indeed and only sea-covered at high-water mark. If you dawdled, and it was a good bay to dawdle through, there were plenty of paths by which you could get up to the cliff path. The only tricky bit was at Telpin, where there was a double cape. The easterly one had an enormous cave in it. It is known as Telpin Church, and it has galleries, windows, even a pulpit. There is a faint tradition that it has been used by persecuted sects, but I think this is a story that has grown up round the name, and I doubt if there is any truth in it. If you reach Telpin Point when the tide is coming in strongly, there is just a chance that you might get caught between the point and the church, but the chance is remote. There is no path here, only cliffs a few hundred feet high. It *could*, if you were *very* careless, catch you out, though, unless there were a very rough sea, it should be possible to scramble high enough at the base of the cliff to keep out of the water. This would give a few hours in which to meditate uncomfortably on the folly of wandering carelessly on unfamiliar coasts.

When cars were much less common than they are nowadays, people used to say that in learning to drive cars the first thing to make sure of was that you knew how to stop them. Similarly, it is a good rule before walking on strange beaches to be sure you know, in case of need, your line of retreat.

Telpin used to be the great spot for catching conger eels. The whole shore is covered with huge rocks, and under the rocks were pools, in some of which the congers stayed between tides. I have caught a little one a few times, but some men skilled at the work, using a barbed crook, occasionally caught six footers, and I have seen some as big as that. It was said that they barked like dogs, but I never heard them. They were vicious brutes with razor-sharp teeth and could give a terrible bite. Of course there were the usual fishermen's yarns, and Luther Phelps always told how a conger bit the toe of his boot clean off. His toes were saved because he was wearing a big pair of somebody else's cast-offs. Now *wasn't* that lucky! Luther fished for anything, anywhere, and I never knew him spoil a good yarn for want of a bit of imagination. All the same, congers had and still have vicious bites.

In the many years I wandered over these beaches there was, and it may still be there today, the wreck of a ship stuck fast in the sand near Ragwin. It stood far below high water and every tide covered it. The gaunt wooden ribs, which were all that were left of it stood bare and tall, weed and barnacle covered, hard as iron, like two long rows of sentinels, with the thicker heavier timbers of bow and stern-post one at each end. That skeleton had been there so long that nobody I ever met knew anything at all about it.

In the wide bay there were a couple of farms. There was a story that many years ago an old farmer and his wife lived alone in one of them, and they supplemented what they made on the barren land by wrecking. They had had a son, but years before he had left home, and they had never heard of him since.

In stormy weather they would lure ships into the bay by putting out lanterns to look as if they were harbour lights. The ships were wrecked, and as the cargoes came ashore they reaped a harvest richer than they ever gathered from the land.

One day after a storm and a shipwreck they were walking the beach in search of what had been washed in, and they came on the body of a sailor, lying face downwards.

"He's alive," said the old woman. "I saw him move."

The old man picked up a heavy rock. "Dead men tell no tales," he said and threw the rock down hard on the sailor's skull.

They turned the body over. It was their long-lost son.

Now this story is told of a number of places along the coast—perhaps of other coasts as well. It is told of a Vaughan of Dunraven Castle (Glamorgan), also of someone at Coity. As it is told, I think the coincidence is a little too contrived. I never de-bunk fairy stories, but the old romances (or horror stories!) about wrecking are not half as romantic as "the tale told in the chimney corner" leads us to believe.

I cannot believe that the captains of ships were so easily lured on to strange coasts by a few lanterns. Lanterns do not necessarily indicate harbours, and, though the ship in which St. Paul travelled to Malta was beached and everyone escaped, that was in daylight, I don't think any captain—not one I have ever known—would run a ship ashore in the dark. In fact the reverse is more likely. Though sailing ships were, and are, driven ashore in storms, any sailor in a sound vessel would prefer to stand out to sea and ride out the storm. It would certainly be safer to be storm-tossed out in the Channel than to come in, say, under the cliffs at Stack Rocks—or at Telpin Point.

What did happen—and on this coast it happened far too often (as it did on the coasts of Devon and Cornwall)—was that sailing boats *were* driven in and wrecked. Local people *did* collect washed-up cargoes, occasionally valuable ones. And it was rare for sailors wrecked on rocky coasts to escape with their lives.

When a sailor did get washed ashore alive, the 'wreckers'—who very, very seldom had caused the wreck (though they may have welcomed it)—were reluctant to touch him or to help him. I do not know who told me this, and it must have been long ago I learned it, but to rescue a man from the sea was unlucky. This belief must go back to some age when saving a life from the sea was considered to be robbing the sea, and the sea would sooner or later take its revenge. And that, I believe, is why from different places you hear the stories of washed-up sailors who have been left to die, or have been actually killed by longshoremen who found them.

The cliffs at Ragwen and Telpin are very high and on the whole are hard, though, as the rocky shore proves, there must have been some notable falls over the centuries. From Telpin to the Pembroke-shire border beyond Black Rocks there is a fine stretch of high cliff in which you can study the strata clearly, but this piece is crumbling away steadily, always has been, and it can only be a matter of time before the cliff gets to the cliff road. There was, the last time I looked, only one narrow field between them. Further west I remember a rough but very good cart road that now lies a hundred feet or so below the present path.

From the cliff road down through from Telpin is a magnificent view of the western end of the bay. Caldy is almost south, then Tenby; Monkstone, two tiny precipitous islands really, thrusts out, then the curve in to Saundersfoot, hugging shelter from the south-westerlies under the hill on its west—but (not so good!) never having a bit of wreckage hurled on to its beach, then the wide sands to Amroth lying a short distance along the road. At the foot of the steep hill is New Inn and the little stream that separates the counties.

And here I must pause a short while, for the view never fails to bring a slight feeling of homesickness. My father was for forty years the village schoolmaster; it was the family home for half a century; some of us still live in the vicinity. It is home.

Begelly, Pembrokeshire
St. Catherine's Island, Tenby, Pembrokeshire

CHAPTER 4

## THE PEMBROKESHIRE COAST

MY mother was not very fond of the sea. Or perhaps it was not so much dislike as distrust. The rest of us loved it, were by it constantly, on it, in it. She had an idea that some day we would all be drowned, which was exactly the fate the landlubber villagers prophesied for us.

When I was about 9, my father built his first boat. He had made little experimental canoes and so on for fun from time to time—the sort of thing you could play with while bathing—but this, though small, was a serious effort. He made it in conventional shape but on the coracle pattern. The stem, keel and stern were heavy oak, mostly chosen, worked and seasoned by himself. Then strong gunwales were fixed, and from this a framework of light ribs that ran both across and from bow to stern. I think he came across difficulties and snags, but he surmounted them. The framework was covered with ships sail canvas and painted many times. The canvas set as hard as a board.

Be patient. I am not writing a family history! All this leads somewhere.

The boat was a complete success. She was as dry inside as a two-hour sermon; she was years old before she let in as much as a spoonful of water. Being broad in the beam she sailed like a duck—that is with more dignity than speed—but, under the lateen sail my Da devised, she sailed well, and it was almost impossible to capsize her. He had little money but lots of ideas and lots of energy. He even made his own oars.

To finish the boat-building story in one go, he built two more boats over the years. The second was canoe shaped, pointed at bow and stern. This was narrow and long, sailed very fast, but was not as stable as number one in heavy seas.

The third, the *Kittiwake*, was the largest and the most ambitious, the same pattern as the first but longer, and this one also sailed fast

Caldy Island from the West
Broad Haven, Pembrokeshire

E

and was stable as well. I expect there are still plenty of people on Carmarthen Bay who remember those boats.

My father, who became as nervous as a stoned sparrow on the roads in his later life, seemed completely fearless in any sort of sea. As I mentioned earlier, all our neighbours predicted drowning as his end. But they were wrong.

Like the mills of God I do seem to go slowly. I can't resist stopping to gossip!

The point about my Daddy's boat is that, being canvas-covered, it was light in weight. That meant a couple of men, or a man and two boys (he and my brother and I), could launch it. We could slide it down a pebble ridge easily, and for when the tide was out he made a trolley. In our village there were two other boats. They were wooden and clinker built and so heavy it took at least twelve men to carry them down to the water. Consequently they hardly ever went out, *sometimes* once a summer, sometimes not. Between Saundersfoot and Laugharne I don't think there was one single boat ever out except ours. That one hardly had time to get dry between trips.

Next, my father slit a lot of long bamboos into narrow strips. These could be bent over hoop fashion from gunwale to gunwale. Over this he fixed some waterproof calico and there you were—a boat with a tent over it. Then we started camping. We would sail along the coast, pull in at evening, or generally before at high tide, haul the boat up above high water, put the tent up, cook our meal and go to bed in the boat. It was not exactly roomy, but, tucked up on the floor of the boat with a twopenny copy of a *Books for the Bairns* and a candle stuck on the nearest seat, I would not, to use a phrase my father often used, have called the king my uncle.

And what I am leading up to is that these childhood experiences gave me a wide and useful knowledge of the inshore waters and a great love for the coast; for the sea, the beaches, the cliffs, the wastes behind them. When I grew older I still liked all these things, and I came to know other waters and other coastlines. I was brought up, you might say, with one foot in the sea.

And that, really, is how I come to be writing this book.

Our second boat was smashed by the sea. She had been hauled up well out of reach of the tide, but in a storm a great wave just licked it up and we didn't even see it again. I don't think there was any great mourning; my father was just hunting for an excuse to start on the *Kittiwake*. I passed a school examination about that time, and he gave me the *Old Tub* for my very own. He would not, though, let me sail her alone, so, though I could manage a boat in almost any conditions, I was not, and never have been, so hot on the art of sailing.

Some coastlines are very irregular—I have the south Cornish coast very much in mind—so that they are made up of a series of capes and a series of inlets, some small, some almost fiords. On such coasts it was usually the custom to make these inlets into harbours. Some are simple, little more than a jetty being built as a breakwater; while others may be quite large, some large and deep enough, like Devonshire's Brixham, to hold large fishing boats. Coasts of this type are noted as centres of the fishing industry. The coast of South Wales, and, indeed, to some extent, all Wales are not among these, and I do not think the people who live on these coasts are great fishermen.

A downright statement like that always lays one open to contradiction, so I had better elaborate. Of course there are fishermen on the Welsh coast, always have been, always will be, but fishing on a really large scale needs harbours, and there are few enough of these on the wide sweeps of land (like Glamorgan) or wide curves of bay (like Carmarthen Bay).

I would like also to qualify what I said earlier about such parts as the Cornish coast. Times have changed. When Stephen Reynolds wrote *Seems So* and Mrs. Havelock Ellis wrote her short stories, fishing was, except for some farming, and when the tin-mines and clay mines were in decline, the *only* Cornish industry. It was a hard life, a dangerous life, and the rewards were poor. Cornishmen may have loved the sea, but if you read some of the old books about Cornwall you soon realise that romance lies in the eye of the beholder. Like the East Anglian fishermen, the trawlermen of Northumbria and the herring catchers of Aberdeen, men went to sea to earn a living not for the fun of it. Nowadays a man can earn more in a short time taking holiday-makers for trips round the bay than he could get in a long time with lines or with nets. The result is that there are less Cornishmen making a living from fishing than there were.

On the Welsh coast there were the fishermen of the Severn and Wye catching the salmon in those baskets known as putchers, fixed out in the stream on larch poles. Whatever Cardiff and Barry did in their early history I have never heard; when they built their docks they were certainly after bigger game than trawlers and fishing boats. From many a village a man may have supplemented the earnings from a smallholding by selling a few fish. There were salmon-fishing coracles on the Towy; still are on the Teifi, where my friend Christmas Evans goes on making a few coracles. At Tenby I seem to remember the days when you could cross the harbour by jumping from trawler to trawler, and Milford had a fine trawling fleet. The men of Solva caught lobsters as big as sharks (or they looked so in a boy's eyes), and north Pembrokeshire had a few coves where you could get a boat to sea.

There is no need to review all the coast in this way. The point is you cannot fish at sea without a boat; you can't take a boat to sea without a small harbour or at the very least a jetty. And, taking the Welsh coast as a whole, there are few of either. To take Carmarthen Bay; eastwards of Saundersfoot there isn't one good place where you could land a catch, or take shelter in bad weather until the Towy, where, if you knew the very tricky channel, you could go upstream to one of the quays at Carmarthen. But from Saundersfoot to Carmarthen is quite a stretch.

Even where fishing was carried on, it has declined to almost nothing in recent years. I don't know when I last saw a trawler in Tenby harbour, and the Milford boats have fallen from a fine fleet to a handful.

All this, of course, brings me back to square one. There was very, very little boating along the coast because you could not get a boat out or in without a lot of bother or a lot of help. But my father managed because he built very light craft.

It was rather strange (still is, I suppose), but the average person living on the coast had very little feeling for the sea, and many really disliked it. Our south Pembrokeshire coastline rose steeply most of the way, and the land was covered either with woods or fertile fields. Farming was the chief industry, and the farmers left the sea alone and hoped it would leave them alone. I could name a dozen farmers in our village—I mean farmers in my day; for all I know they may go water-skiing now—who had never bathed or even paddled in their lives. They would send a cart to the beach for a load of stones from the pebble ridge; and the same cart might fetch clay from the exposed clay banks around the submerged forest, but that was about the extent of their interest. As I have already mentioned, they considered my father an eccentric because he liked being in the sea or on the sea. I don't think there were half a dozen men in the parish who could swim. A few boys learned—they were forsaking the sober habits of their fathers and going bathing—when they got a break from the work in hayfield or cornfield, but some of my friends, tough young hearties who could drive a horse and cart or mow a field of hay or ride a frisky horse, were not allowed by their anxious mothers to go out in our boat.

But there is a queer contradiction. Most of the villages had a sort of fair or feast day some time in the summer. Some of the towns have them still: St. Margaret's Fair in Tenby, Porfield Fair in Haverfordwest, Narberth and Whitland Fairs, that were hiring fairs for farm labourers in the old days. Amroth had nothing quite as grand as that, but it did have its day of jollification. It was held on the last Friday in August and was called Big Day. It was held when I was young, but I am going back into other people's memories for what I have to relate next (though a few of those people are still alive). I suppose by Big Day pretty well all the farms would have completed the hay harvest and some if not all of the corn harvest as well. So the inland farms made a yearly holiday of Amroth Big Day. They loaded their carts and gambos (open farm carts) with eatables and drinkables, left a skeleton staff at home for milking, and with the rest of the household set off for the sea. They started the night before, and all night long (this is what my dear gossips told me) there would be one long unending procession down the lanes to the sea. The local people would often sit up on the warm summer night to watch them go by.

And so on Big Day the beaches, the pebble ridge, the sands were covered with people, who feasted and drank and paddled and slept in the sun and generally had a gay old time.

Then they bathed. And—this I have been assured by more than one person is the truth—they all, men, women and children, stripped mother naked and plunged into the sea.

When I heard these stories we had run into a more puritanical age, and it did not seem possible. But it did happen. Prudishness is often only an exaggeration of the current taste. I am almost sure there is a reference somewhere in Kilvert's diary to bathing in the nude.

By the time I was a youngster the aforesaid puritanical age had arrived and was going strong. Even my father, who by no means kept all the rules, would not have taken out his boat on a Sunday. On

Sunday we did not paddle nor walk on the sands, and bathing was right out of the question, though many of us youngsters swam in some hidden cove. On a Sunday there were things you could do and could not do, and mostly you could not. Farming customs, even among the most godly, are liberal enough these days, but not even the most anxious farmer with half a field of hay out and rain threatening for Monday would have dared risk the wrath of God by carting it on the Sabbath. If you had failed to get in enough potatoes on Saturday for Sunday dinner you jolly-well went short. To be seen digging them on that day would have scandalised the whole parish.

"To be seen", those are the significant words. Of course, though there were people who really did think it a sin to do on Sunday anything not absolutely necessary, there was also a cartload of hypocrisy to which everyone added his quota.

I remember well my mother telling me to cut a cabbage for dinner one Sunday morning.

"Keep down", she said, meaning don't let myself be seen over the garden wall. "Mind Mrs. Phillips doesn't see you."

Mrs. Phillips was our nearest neighbour and one of my mother's best friends. But she must not see any of us cut a cabbage on Sunday!

Greatly daring, for argument with grown-ups was not encouraged, I ventured a question.

"God can see me. Why does it matter what the neighbours see when He knows?"

"You do what I tell you," said my mother. "God is a lot more understanding than the neighbours."

In matters of convention my mother conformed. My father, while avoiding the most deadly sins like boating and fishing, seemed to take a wicked delight in trying to shock the village.

As a rule he did it very successfully.

If this sort of thing concerned only our own village and district it would be material for a very localised history. But it did not. You could hear similar tales of any sport from Chepstow to Chester.

With fishing the same. What we did I think most seaside villages and towns did. Lobsters and crabs we did not have, though Tenby fishermen did, and they were caught from there pretty well up to the Cardiganshire coast, where the steep rocky seabeds gave way again to wide sandy beaches.

We caught mackerel in summer, and if shoals came into the bay one of the other village boats (if they could find a dozen men to carry her down) might put out. The Saundersfoot and Tenby boats, of course, reaped a rich harvest. I have lost my taste for fishing, and a fish leaping and threshing through the water with a hook in its mouth is no longer a pleasurable excitement. But as a boy I loved it, and if you got right into a shoal you could pull the mackerel in with as many on the line as there were hooks on it. Almost as good was to look into the clear water and spy what we called mackerel bait, tiny fishes like small sprats, hurrying along in a narrow column like soldiers on the march. Miles of them it seemed. My father said these were what the mackerel came in for. I don't know whether he was guessing, but when the shoal got among the mackerel bait there was a great commotion in the water and a lot of leaping out of it.

The flocks of gulls enjoyed it too.

In rough seas a few of the village men went fishing from the beach for bass as the tide came in. For bait they used lug-worms they dug out of the sand, and, though some men stood for hours with never a catch, others would have perhaps half a dozen bass many pounds in weight.

Many of the village men set out a night line, fixing it down at the ebb and inspecting it twelve hours later. The snag in this kind of fishing was that often an early catch was eaten by a bigger fish. Sometimes this ended in catastrophe for the robber. I remember my buddy (when we had not had a quarrel) Jack Smith, the Castle gardener's son, catching a big conger, inside which was a small fish (a herring I think). Presumably, inside the herring was the bait.

Stop nets were usually made of wire netting. They were fixed to iron stakes driven into the sand, and in shape were like a U with the open mouth landwards. At certain times a lot of fish, mainly plaice, would find themselves stranded in the stop nets.

A drag-net worked on the same principle, but was hard labour. The net, ordinary fish net of course and the longer the better, was attached to two strong poles. One man waded into the sea to armpit depth; another took the other pole. Then they walked along slowly and the net like an enormous deep bow followed them. Every few hundred yards the chap in the water came ashore and they pulled the net up on to the sand. When fish were plentiful the catches could be enormous, and it was usual to hire Billy Hugh's donkey cart to carry the fish.

Billy Hugh was William Hugh Lewis, an eccentric, deaf, with a speech impediment, who was one of our local 'characters', and we had quite a few of those. His donkey cart was about the only available mode of transport, especially when the farmers had all their horses at work. It was quite fun to hire Billy's cart, and adventurous also because often the donkey would not go at all, though there were other occasions when it went all too well.

My mother was very fond of hiring Billy Hugh's donkey cart, and I remember once her having it to take me and my brother and Mrs. Dawkins—local baby-sitter, gossip and lonely wives' companion to all the parish—for a picnic to Pendine. On Marros Plain, some way before the church, my mother and I got out to pick some flowers. The donkey wasn't such a fool as he was thought to be. The load was halved, and he decided it was a good time to continue the journey. My mother and I ran after the cart, shouting; the donkey broke into a gallop, an event almost unheard of; my brother sat on the floor of the cart. Mrs. Dawkins sat on the board across the cart, holding the reins but not having the remotest idea what to do with them, as upright as a post, very dignified, for all the world like a French aristocrat being hurried to the guillotine. It wouldn't have mattered, but in a few hundred yards there was the almost precipitous hill down to Green Bridge. Happily for all of us, the donkey decided that galloping was not in his line.

The other historic time my family shared with Billy's donkey was when we had some relations visiting us and my mother, as usual, hired the donkey cart to take them to the station at Kilgetty to catch the train for Tenby. As was not unusual, the donkey would not go, and my mother sent for Billy to come and help. He got them to the station and, when they came home, met them. They treated him so generously that he got horribly drunk, and though normally he was completely under the domination of his wife, he went home, rebelled and turned out all the summer visitors they had staying in the house. It must have been a very inconvenient and uncomfortable time for the lodgers, but later it made joyful telling and was considered uproariously funny.

What happened to all the queer characters and eccentrics we had? Perhaps they are there still, and we do not notice them. But all small communities looked inwards then, and we made the most of what fun we had on the doorstep. I doubt if there was a daily newspaper in any house in the village, and such news as there was filtered in slowly, perhaps carried by the postman, and no doubt a few papers were brought home on Narberth Market Day or by somebody who ventured as far as Tenby on a Saturday.

The most extraordinary fishing I ever saw took place in the summer of 1917 and was repeated in the exact pattern in 1918. It started when someone who was bathing kept stepping on large flatfish. There were so many that a few bright spirits went up to the village and got garden forks. With these, they entered the water again, and when they felt a fish they speared it. The result was that they caught a large number of fish. Of course the news got around, and next day half the villagers who could spare the time were in the sea jabbing away with garden forks and pitch forks. Even more fish were caught, and men carried them off in sacks. Word got to Saundersfoot and Tenby, and their fishermen arrived in their boats. A few enterprising men, my father among them, got Bill Beynon the blacksmith to make barbed spearheads for them. It was a most extraordinary sight. Half a parish up to the middle in the warm summer sea jabbing left, right and centre and lifting enormous fish out of the water on the prongs of, say, a hay-fork. Fish could be had for the asking, and our tailor—we had village tailors then—gave me more than I could carry.

You see I had no fish. With the best intention in the world I fished, but, like better men before my time, I toiled but I caught nothing. As soon as I stepped on a fish I stepped off even quicker. My feet were ticklish.

This, free-for-all fishing happened again the next summer. And, as far as I know, it never happened again. What drove the shoals in in that queer fashion nobody ever knew; though, as you may guess, theories helped many a friendly pint of beer on its way.

By a strange coincidence I came across this passage in a book published in 1913,* "The fishermen of the Traeth Bach catch much flat-fish by spearing, and it is interesting to watch the men wade into the water up to their chests in pursuit of their quarry."

Perhaps our spear-fishing was not unique after all. Or perhaps the north Merionethshire fishermen, as we did, reaped (while Mr. Morris happened to be around) an unexpected harvest.

The anthracite coal measure, a rather thin seam, was visible in the strata of the cliffs on each side of the village, and there had been small coal workings; the relics of them, including some rather dangerous pit shafts, could be found in the fields overlooking the

* *Merionethshire* by A. Morris, Cambridge County Geographies.

bay. This coal was private property—just as well perhaps, because any open-cast working on the cliff seam would have in time caused some terrific falls of rock. Rather less understandable was the fact that the coal was still private property even when a high tide had washed some out and it lay about on the beach. More than one unfortunate on the look-out for cheap fuel found himself fined in court for 'stealing' coal from the beach.

Further west the coal was mined at the little colliery at Bonville's Court and carried to Saundersfoot Harbour in open 'trams', pulled by such a tiny 'Puffing Billy' of an engine as would bring tears of joy to any modern steam-train enthusiast. The little railway ran along the face of the cliffs from Wiseman's Bridge to Saundersfoot and passed through one medium-length tunnel and two short ones. Officially nobody was supposed to use the tunnels, but everybody did. As a first safeguard you asked at local cottages when the train would come. As a second—everybody knew the technique—if a train caught you in a tunnel, you turned and hared back the way you had come as fast as you could. My friend, the aforesaid Jack Smith, ignored the second precaution one day when he was wheeling his bicycle over the sleepers towards Saundersfoot. He heard the train coming and ran forward instead of back. Train and boy met right at the tunnel entrance. Jack managed to squeeze back against the tunnel wall. His bicycle was less fortunate, and the engine twisted it into what would pass for a very *avant-garde* bit of metal sculpture.

That was the only casualty I ever heard of.

"There is a character of active bustle seldom to be found elsewhere in the district", a visitor wrote of Saundersfoot in 1861. "Up to 1835 the coal was taken from carts on the beach by boat, and as many as thirty ships might be loading at a time. In 1833 5,817 tons of coal were exported and 5,680 tons of culm. In 1859, with the harbour in use, the trade had grown to 16,755 tons of coal and 16,595 tons of culm."

There is a seam of iron-ore also in the cliffs, and west of Amroth this was worked on the Patches. Nobody seemed to know why the 'Patches', but a very old friend (I mean very much older than I) said each man who mined ore had a 'patch' of his own. She also told me that Spanish boats came for the ore, and it was carried out to them in rowing boats. Spanish boats coming to Pembrokeshire for iron-ore is a coals-to-Newcastle sort of story, but, if true, there must be a reason; the ore may have had some special property. I heard later that iron-ore was also shipped from Saundersfoot.

Well, that is one peasant industry that is surely at an end for ever, but the ruins of a blacksmith's forge still stands above high-water mark; and the heavy brown iron-ore pebbles still bounce remarkably well, thrown hard against the neighbouring rocks.

The 'wrecking' at Amroth followed the same pattern roughly as that practised all round the coast. As I stated earlier and for the reasons stated, I rather discount the stories of lights being used to lure ships ashore. Even less credible are the stories of lanterns tied under the necks of cows, if only because they are much too sensible to wander about on cliff fields on stormy nights. Of course there was some villainy; some squires claimed that anything thrown up on their foreshore was their property. In Gower that claim led to what was practically a battle between the Mansels and the Herberts over a ship wrecked near Oxwich on the day after Christmas in 1557. In the fight over the spoils an old lady, Anne Mansell, was killed by a stone thrown by a Herbert supporter. The result was a Star Chamber trial, and Sir George Herbert had to pay a large fine.

And there was from time to time what amounted practically to piracy in the Channel. But that is another thing altogether, and at times (depending on who the victims were) piracy was a respectable calling.

The whole coast, from beginning to end, varied a lot in the amount of wreckage thrown up. Sheltered havens would have hardly a stick of firewood, while under a cape like Telpin or Ragwen, open to the southerly gales, there would be cartloads. Most of it was not much use for anything but firewood, and 'picking sticks off the beach' was a gentle pastime followed by old ladies and children, and half a winter's firing could be collected by cottagers in that way. I say cottagers because farmers had all the firewood they wanted nearer home. Sometimes useful timber—doors, ship's hatches, beams and so on—were washed in. After a storm, men with no more urgent business on hand wandered the beaches for miles, generally starting at dawn. If they found anything they wanted they pulled it up above high-water mark and put a stone, usually a largish stone, on it. That stone was the sign that that particular bit of jetsam was somebody else's property. I expect we had a few light-fingered lads around—what place has not?—but that unwritten law about never taking anything with a stone on it was never broken. I should know because once, before I understood the custom properly, I kicked a stone off a ship's hatch and, with a great struggle, dragged it to one of our farm neighbours and sold it for the almost unheard wealth of half a crown. As soon as my parents found out what I had done I had to give back the half-crown, collect the hatch and return it to where it belonged. And that was a mile away.

Ah well, some people have to learn the hard way!

There were men who built garden sheds and outhouses of 'wreck', but as a rule what came in was not wildly exciting. If you could find a barrel of port wine you got a very large sum in salvage. Twice I knew that to happen but I was not even near the finders. I imagine most containers of that sort would be pounded to pieces on the stones, for barrel staves were often washed in. One man found a little cask of whisky and got more in salvage than most workers earned in years. We all knew we had to look out for ambergris, but since nobody I ever heard of even knew what the stuff looked like there was not a lot of point in looking. I have seen cases of onions and oranges strewn over the pebble ridge between Telpin and Ragwen, but they were salted and completely uneatable. My mother once soaked what seemed passable oranges and made marmalade of them, but that was uneatable also.

Any find that seemed likely to pay dividends in salvage money was reported; the others were not. Some men did not even know what salvage was. The sons of a farmer between Telpin and Marros once found a ship's boat. The coastguards got to hear of this and, perhaps as a hint, sent to the finders to ask if they wanted to claim salvage. The boys said, no thanks, they'd had all the salvage they wanted. So they had; they had chopped up the boat and used it for firewood.

Then there was the mysterious rowing-boat, about sixteen feet I would say, from memory, that lay under a hedge one field away from our house. I particularly remember that because it was foreign-looking, flat-bowed (instead of coming to a pointed prow), something like the cod-fishing dories I had seen in pictures in my *Captains Courageous*. Nobody could, or would, tell me where or when or how it got there, a mile from the beach, though it was in fair condition then. I played games in it for a while, then got tired of them, and the grass and the brambles grew over it and through it, and it was forgotten, presumably even by the men who put it there.

Once, at the end of the First World War, a number of mustard-gas containers were washed in, and, though they were metal, some men got them open. That was not at all funny.

I seem to remember a mine at Wiseman's Bridge and an old gentleman who would keep poking at it with his walking stick! He and that great ugly sphere were alone together in no time.

The best wrecking story dates also from the end of the First World War. My father, my brother and I were camping (in a tent) on Telpin Farm. In a small sectional building always and everywhere known as The Bungalow were Harry Shellard, a dentist from Cardiff, and his brother-in-law, Jim McGuire, who came from London. They, and sometimes their families, came every summer for surely thirty years or more. Shellard (who recently died in his nineties) and my father were both keen amateur painters; McGuire was a good musician—so was my father—so we all got on wonderfully together.

One stormy morning it was found I had a chill so they put me to bed in The Bungalow and then all went down to bathe in the surf. In no time at all Brother Roy was back, wild with excitement.

"They've found a barrel of port washed in", he announced. Now that *was* news, enough to cure me of chills or any other ailments, but he added the sad news that somebody had already found it and had put a stone on it.

However, port is port, and the Customs and Excise were not likely to miss one small taste out of it so Roy had come to get a bottle and a gimlet.

I had a double misfortune to bear now: I felt like something the cat had brought in, *and* I had to miss the fun of seeing that lovely thick plum-coloured liquid trickling into a bottle.

But the liquid never did trickle into the bottle. My Da with his auger he bored a little hole—I hope you know the song "The Golden Vanity"—but nothing happened. The conspirators decided that there was no air pressure in the cask, and they bored another little hole; again nothing happened. They bored lots of little holes, but out of that great heavy container not one trickle of port would come. Then one of them noticed how greasy the gimlet had become.

The barrel was full of lard!

Quite a number of barrels of lard floated in. Chunks of the stuff from broken barrels also washed up, and you could pick up lumps as big as footballs covered with seaweed, sand and bits of stick.

Useless, of course, but it was great for lighting fires. Then some bright lad (or his wife) had an idea. They heated a big boiler of water and dropped some of the dirty mess in it. When it melted the sand and pebbles dropped to the bottom of the boiler while sticks and seaweed floated. This was skimmed off and there was left some pure lard. Fat, good edible fat, was rationed then and in very short supply. The barrels were still coming in on every tide. But—what a strange coincidence—*all* the barrels from then on were smashed and useless for salvage! The people used to go and collect it by the pailful. There was not much salvage claimed on lard barrels, but, my word, you should have seen the rows and rows of jars of good cooking fat on the shelves of every pantry in the parish.

A mile or so along the shore is the little hamlet of Wiseman's Bridge. At least it was a little hamlet, though the last time I went through it looked like growing into a holiday town. There was, about a century ago, a wise man, or sorcerer living at the bridge. His name was Prout, and I have heard stories of some of the wonderful cures he worked. The place, however, got its name from a much earlier healer, for there has been an inn on that spot for over 300 years at least.

When I was a youngster Wiseman's Bridge was kept by a couple, a brother and sister called James. I had to think hard to remember that surname because it was Sarah the Bridge and Ben the Bridge. The place was little more than an alehouse with a small holding, and a very modest one at that. It had no bar. If you called there for a glass of beer you drank it in the kitchen like everybody else. My father seldom passed the bridge without dropping in, and many a pleasant half-hour have I spent on the settee in that little kitchen warming my toes at a glowing culm fire. The culm was anthracite slack mixed with wet clay. A culm fire took hours to burn up and many more hours to die down. Some hardly ever went out.

If my mother was with us she too came into the kitchen and sipped a genteel nip of whisky; I, if in luck, had a marble-stoppered bottle of pop, but that was a luxury. If there were men drinking—there were never more than two or three at a time—my mother and Sarah sat in the back-kitchen and exchanged whispered confidences in the candlelight. Women did not sit drinking where men were. I believe there was a polite convention that they did not drink at all.

Sarah and Ben were more of our 'characters'. They were good, possibly poor but certainly kind people. Sarah, in voluminous petticoats always curtsied to her 'betters', and very gracefully she did it too. I remember Ben as toothless, but he managed the feat of holding a clay pipe in bare gums very well.

A more celebrated character was a certain Davy, who lived between the bridge and Stepaside. He celebrated his early eighties by getting two young women pregnant. To cap this they lived about ten miles away, and Davy's vigour did not include walking.

"Davy!" reproached the rector when the news got around. "How could you! How *could* you!"

"Oh, it was no trouble at all, Reverend," said Davy cheerfully. "I borrowed Tom Absolom's pony."

And Tom was another! It was he the rector found in a ditch sleeping off the overnight beer!

"Drunk again, Tom," said the rector.

"So'm I, sir," said Tom.

It was always the rector and Tom. On another similar occasion the rector said, "What would you say if you found *me* in this disgusting condition?"

"Never a mot to a soul, sir," said Tom.

The queer bit about that story is the dialect use of the French *mot* (pronounced *mott* locally) for word. It is the only French word I remember hearing in a locality quite rich in a distinctive speech of its own, though Saunders who gave its name to Saundersfoot, came over (reputedly) with the Conqueror; and de Bonville, whose name still lives in Bonville's Court was Norman.

Saundersfoot Harbour was pretty busy when I first knew it. Small steamers and schooners came in steadily, for the anthracite coal I suppose, and perhaps iron-ore. I never heard of any other cargo, though an old book I have mentions iron-ore and white marble. Where they found white marble near Saundersfoot I have no idea. Then that trade died out, and for years the harbour was very quiet indeed. There were more boys bathing than boats. Now it seems to be full again, mainly of pleasure craft of one sort and another. The whole coast has changed so much that at times I hardly seem to know it, yet the bones of the place are the same, and out of the holiday season the changes are less apparent. On the shore I can even find pools I played in as a child.

Beyond Saundersfoot the change is less obvious because the cliffs rise again and there is less sand and no beach at high tide. The two great humps of Monkstone rear inhospitably out of the sea. When we rowed or sailed to Tenby, if the sea was calm my father would go between the two and through crystal clear water we could see the barnacle-encrusted rocks not so very far below. A few times we slept on the pebble ridge beyond Monkstone—Tremayne Sands, I think it was called—and on one occasion I started to climb the outer Monkstone to see if it was true that a hermit once lived on it. But halfway up it became too difficult, and the bottom did look a long way down so I went back. There were places the cliffs could be climbed, and in a few places I did climb them, not without some risk, though I did not realise that at the time.

I had a better head for heights then than I have now, but I think I was cured of rock-climbing the day I got home and showed my father some hawk's eggs I had collected. I'm sorry to say I was one of those horrid boys who collected birds' eggs: only-one-out-of-each-nest-the-bird-can't-count sort of thing.

"Where did you get those?" asked my father.

"Tom and Sidney (two equally horrid little boys) let me down the quarry on a rope."

"Better not mention it to your mother", said my Daddy drily. "Jones the Shop was doing exactly the same thing on the cliffs beyond Giltar Point this afternoon, and he fell and was killed".

Even horrid little boys can think—sometimes!

I seem to remember getting from Monkstone to Waterwynch at low tide though it meant some rather rough scrambling; but Waterwynch to Tenby at one particular spot always defeated me, though I tried more than once. There are cliff paths everywhere, though, and I think you could walk, given the energy, from Pendine to Tenby without setting foot on a road. Of course our boating holidays gave me a wonderful chance to learn every foot of the coast in my own area. Fancy pulling up a small open boat on Tenby sands and sleeping in it these days. Yet that is just what we did.

"Tenbeigh", said Daniel Defoe, "the most agreeable town on all the sea coast of South Wales, except Pembroke." Not everybody would agree to the one exception. Tenby has had its ups and downs. It started—considering it as a town—mainly for fishing, with perhaps a little gentlemanly piracy thrown in. No doubt, being fortified from quite early times it was a useful military strongpoint as well. But when Giraldus Cambrensis was rector the tithe was mainly of fish. Much of St. Mary's Church is thirteenth-century, and it is one of the most interesting in the county or anywhere along

Milford trawler, Pembrokeshire
Aberaeron Harbour, Cardiganshire

the coast. Flemings settled here, and there is some Flemish buildings or Flemish evidence in some of the older buildings, but the old story that they practically took possession of the town will not hold water. Tombs in the church date from about 1400, and if there are any purely Flemish ones I have not seen them. The tomb of Thomas White gives his wives their maiden names, which was very much a Welsh custom. The Whites were merchants of the fifteenth century, and Thomas and brother John must have had a finger in every Tenby pie for a very long time, for between them they were mayor thirteen times. Thomas gave refuge to a 14-year old Henry Tudor after the Battle of Tewkesbury. When Henry became Henry VII after Bosworth he paid his debt.

The kneeling effigy is of a later Mayor, William Risam, and the crack near the head was made by the bullet of a Roundhead soldier. One account I have says Oliver Cromwell was the marksman. Why ever a Roundhead should want to shoot a man at his prayers is not clear, but the story is a good one. Let it rest.

Another tablet commemorates an early mathematician, Dr. Robert Recorde, who invented (if that is the right word) the 'equals' sign, which of course is =. Not exciting but men have been remembered for less worthy reasons.

Much of the old town wall still looks strong, and the Five Arches, three of them comparatively recent, is picturesque and sturdy. But the fortifications on Castle Hill are, if also picturesque, quite ruinous. They took a beating more than once in the town's history, but Cromwell is blamed for their final overthrow. The paths around them give views that can hardly be bettered; on a clear day you can see the great sweep of the bay from Gower all the way round. Lundy is southwards; St. Catherine's, an island at high tide, is just below, once a fort but a fort no longer; and Caldy with its Benedictine Monastery lies only a mile or so away across current-torn Caldy Sound. The currents between Giltar Point and the smaller St. Margaret's Island are apparent even to the naked eye, especially with a good fresh wind. The water can look very angry here. Tenby and its sands (the popular North Sands hidden by the town) lie behind, and a rocky inhospitable coast to the west. At least, that is what for years I was led to believe. I was very strongly discouraged in my youth to go beyond Tenby; Caldy Sound was definitely out of bounds. But later I found it was not such a fearful stretch after all. Between Tenby and St. Ann's Head, which is north of the

The Melindwr Valley, near Aberystwyth, Cardiganshire

F

entrance to Milford Haven, is some of the finest cliff scenery in the British Isles. In a series of great promontories they rise, many of them sheer from the sea, hundreds of feet high, open to the Atlantic and the prevailing sou'westerlies, and there seems hardly a day in the year that there is not enough wind to raise a swell that smashes into foam at the base of the cliffs. A wind, without attaining anything near gale force can rise here quickly enough to start quite sizeable breakers, and, I have always understood, there are some tricky currents in places. No indeed, it was not a piece of coastline on which to encourage a boy to go boating.

But the idea I once had of an unbroken line of formidable and dangerous cliffs was quite wrong. From Lydstep Cove to Milford Haven there are some lovely beaches. The motor car has now found its way to many of them, and caravans are not unknown, nor camping sites. I do not complain; I would not even had I any right to. If we are given leisure then we must search out the most delightful spots to spend our leisure. But a little kindly control is not out of place at times. It is, I believe, exercised when necessary, but if the poor are not today always with us (in this country), the litter problem is.

Mind you, not all the pleasant little coves have been discovered, and a few are inaccessible to anything on wheels.

In the area between the coast and, roughly, Milford Haven and the eastern River Cleddau the country is nearly all quiet. Much is unspoiled and perfect. Some is spoiled and imperfect due to army training and the ruins of old W.D. buildings. It is incredible that the Mother of Parliaments can make laws to stop people throwing rubbish down, yet leave so much of her own lying about. But there is beauty untouched and the lanes are small enough and narrow enough to discourage any motorist. These are the places for the people not in a hurry—which anyhow is nearly always the worst thing in the world to be in—and if you like trees (a bit wind-swept at times!), green fields, the loveliest wild flowers from celandine and primrose time until the hawthorn berries redden in autumn, birds in infinite variety, then here is the place to search for them.

One thought leads to another. Along the coast there is an enormous variety of seabirds, some common, some not. I know all the usual crowd—the gulls, guillemots, puffins, cormorants, oystercatchers, kittiwakes—and can recognise a few more that feed on the foreshore or in the inland marshes further north. But the expert on seabirds here is R. M. Lockley, and he has lived among them and studied them and written about them for so long that it is wise for lesser naturalists to hold their peace. As the silly old cliché said: you open your mouth and you put your foot into it. So I had better keep off subjects I know so much less about than Mr. Lockley does.

But if you want an unequalled view of seabirds, common and rare, great and small, visit the Stack Rocks which you can see from the cliffs south of Castlemartin and Warren. There, with a pair of good field-glasses, you can have perfect bird-watching from dawn to dusk with no trouble at all. Go, of course, when there is not much south-west wind—that could sometimes mean quite a wait—and go in spring when the birds are breeding.

There is, by the way, another Stack, further north in St. Bride's Bay, but I do not know which, if any, seabirds breed there. They do on many of the larger islands, and, with permission, visitors may visit them, but again we are on R. M. Lockley's territory; his study of Manx Sheerwaters on Skokholm for instance is part of ornithological history.

From Tenby the coast lanes lead to all sorts of interesting spots. There is Penally with its ancient churchyard cross. Lydstep Haven is a lovely little bay guarded from land by tall cliffs and at sea by the Caldy Sound currents. Manorbier has one of the most interesting churches in the country, while the fine old castle is the ruin of the one in which Giraldus Cambrensis, writer, scholar, wit, cleric and handsome young man—he said so himself—was born. How he loved Manorbier: "Penbroch, the finest part of the province of Demetia; and the place I have just described, the most delightful part of Penbroch. It is evident, therefore, that Manor Pirr is the pleasantest spot in Wales".

His best known writing is the *Itinerary Through Wales*, in which he described Archbishop Balwin's progress as he preached the crusade in the country. He was gossipy but very shrewd. He was a success in most things but his greatest ambition, to become Bishop of St. David's, he just failed to achieve.

Though he called himself 'the Welshman' he was only partly Welsh. Perhaps it was the charming part, since his grandmother, Nest, was one of the greatest beauties of her time, though her virtue was not always as faultless as her looks. Lamphey where there was once a Bishop's palace is a mile or two inland, but back on the coast you can go down to St. Govan's Head and the tiny ancient chapel

near the sea. A long flight of steps leads down to this primitive place
of worship, and they say you can never count the same number of
steps coming up as going down. A narrow ravine Huntsman's Leap
is not far away, and a few miles westwards the Stack Rocks, where
the cliff scenery is magnificent. All the villages around are charming
and at Bosherston are Bosherston pools, a sort of inland mere where
water lilies grow by the thousand, and from there you can go round
or across the narrow peninsular to Angle on its little bay and then
we are in Milford Haven.

The Haven is varied, so full of history, ancient lore, villages,
natural history that it needs a volume of its own. There may be one
or two natural harbours in the world as good, but this fjord with
its gentle hilly shores is surely unique on our side of the world.

In strength may lie weakness, and the Haven's wonderful
properties as a sheltered roadstead make up the reason why the great
oil companies have arrived with their refining plants, their chimneys,
their Heath-Robinson tangle of pipes and pumps and storage tanks.
A lot of people dislike these.

But let's be fair! What they have done they have done as decently
as they could. They are concentrated in a comparatively small area.
From many places—from most parts of the Haven—they are not in
sight, and, which is the most important I suppose, they bring money
and work to an area that has not had too much of either since
Pembroke Dock closed its shipyards. I go very often to this area and
I hardly notice them any more. I have an idea that the refineries do
not dominate the Haven; it is the Haven that is absorbing them.

"Their money's useful!" said a Pembrokeshire county councillor
drily. "Scenery's no good in an empty pay packet".

As for the tankers—well, the Haven is just the place to show up
the big ships for what small fish they really are. As long as they
don't spill any cargo!

You can go along Milford Haven (the haven) on each side by
good roads, or, a mile or less from the water, along winding country
lanes. If you go up by boat you perhaps get a better idea of the coast.
It is a great yachting centre, and, sheltered from the open sea though
it may be, the westerly wind can stir it up to be quite lively at times.
On a calm day a row up to Lawrenny say from Milford Haven (the
town) is not an over-strenuous exercise. A motor-boat is quicker
but the sound of water dripping off oar-blades is a pleasanter sound
than the angry waspish screaming of an outboard motor.

Long ago Milford was hardly even a village. It grew and sent out its whaling fleets; when they stopped the trawlers filled its harbours; now most of those also have gone. But it is a pleasant town, and the street above the water—wisely without a house on its southern side—is about as nice a sea-town walk as you could find anywhere. They built ships here once; battleships were made at Pembroke Dock, and the first ironclad (they told me at 'The Jolly Sailer' in Burton it was the first) is anchored just opposite Burton. All the way the villages come down to the water's edge, nearly always with their churches discreetly inland (remember the Scandinavian pirates and Vikings had a liking for this stretch of water), and little streams come to join the main flood. But the two Cleddaus, Eastern and Western are the main feeders, one coming under the once formidable walls of Haverfordwest Castle, one turning from stream to estuary just below Canaston Bridge.

Around Canaston Bridge are woods, but they seem not much more than scrubland compared with the Canaston Woods with their mighty oaks that grew there when I was at school in Narberth. A few times we played truant to explore it on Friday afternoons, and once three of us got mildly lost on a summer day. That was the day we found a deserted church—right in the middle of the forest; no roof, no windows, no furnishings of any kind: only four walls and a tower given over to the nesting jackdaws. Nobody ever seemed to know anything about it; nobody could tell us anything about it. I would say it might be a dream but it is marked 'church' in Gothic script on the ordnance map though no place name is attached. It was like the church in Burns' *Tam O'Shanter*:

Kirk-Alloway was drawing nigh,
Where ghaists and houlets nightly cry.

I don't suppose any of us who clambered among the ruins so bravely in the sunshine would have gone there at night. I don't know that I would now!

That day I learned a snake could climb. We started it, a great yard-long length of wonderfully marked grass snake, and when we gave chase it went up into the bushes and ran through the branches as if it had a hundred legs. Oh yes, snakes can climb, and they can swim too, wriggling through the water, head erect, at a great rate, and I remember one that escaped us in Ludchurch deserted quarry pools by taking to the water.

Most of the Haven villages are delightful, and a few are deserted, though not in the decayed sense of Goldsmith's Auburn. One that fascinates me is St. Ishmael's (not to be confused with the one in Carmarthenshire), not so much for the village itself as for the little church at the bottom of a narrow lane, the enormous old house (rectory or vicarage), the path through the snowdrop woods to the sea, and then an enormous high wall built right across the cove. Built by whom? For what reason? Just a gentleman's private beach someone said, private no more for the great gateway in the wall is doorless; but if anyone ever did want to do a bit of smuggling in the Haven, this would be the spot for it.

Dale, where Henry Tudor landed to become Henry VII, is at the end of the peninsula, a perfect little bay for yachtsmen, and then you can go either to St. Ann's Head, or through Marloes (where the smugglers were called Marloes Gulls) to Wooltack Point, where you can look over the tormented currents to the islands of Skomer and Skokholm.

St. Bride's Bay swings in a deep arc from Wooltack to St. David's and another fascinating island, Ramsey. Out to sea from Ramsey are the cruel rocky islets called Bishop and Clerks. George Owen, the Elizabethan writer on Pembrokeshire said they "preached deadly doctrines to their winter audience, such poor seafaring men as are forcyd thether by tempest; onlie in one thing they are to be commended, they keepe residence better than the rest of the canons of that see are wont to do".

Indeed, it was a poor prospect for any vessel that got as far inshore as this, yet the crew of a Swedish ship, wrecked on the Bishops in 1780 got on to one of the smaller islets, were seen through a spy-glass by a Mrs. Williams of Trelyddin, and were all saved.

The cliffs of St. Bride's Bay are almost as fine as those on the southern coast, and to my mind are not as unscalable. At least, to me they do look as if you could get up out of reach of the tide if you were caught. In between the cliffs are beaches, tiny coves as at Little Haven, wide sweeping sandy beaches like those of Broad Haven (there is a Broad Haven east of St. Govan's head, also, by the way) and Newgale where the Atlantic rollers run in, in lines of white foam so straight they might have been drawn along a ruler's edge. Solva is different—a little fjord winding in to a quay, and the old cottages and houses dotted all over the steep hills, that make the village quite unlike any on the coast, in the county or out of it.

A good place to buy a fresh lobster is Solva, a holiday village, but it has had its day as a lively little port, though for what cargoes nobody seems quite certain. It was probably lime or Precelly stone. Perhaps some Welsh homespun as well, for White Mill, a little way upstream was still working the last time I saw it, the only village mill I should think in Wales that is as busy as when it was built.

From St. David's, the tiny city and ancient cathedral in the hollow—presumably so that it would be out of sight of Vikings, pirates or any other thievish seamen—the coast twists its way up to Strumble Head, cliffs everywhere and sandy little bays, and here and there a small, generally deserted harbour or quay. Narrow lanes thread their way to and fro and lead to or nearly to the beaches, places like Porthgain, Trevine and Abercastle. Behind, in the south, the hills of Pembrokeshire brag themselves as mountains under the title Mynydd Prescelly*; magic hills, boulder-strewn, with menhirs and cromlechs. It was busy enough here thousands of years ago when they quarried the smaller stones for Stonehenge, where the hairy engineers of the time worked out how they should be taken on the long journey to Wiltshire. But the Precelly slopes always return to their primitive loneliness, and their old customs. Why, I know a few farms that still celebrate *Old* New Year's Day on 12th January and have a real old Welsh *Nosen Lawen* in honour of the festival.

And then they say Pembrokeshire isn't Welsh!

Between Strumble Head and Fishguard is Careg-Gwastad Point, and in the bay under it a French invasion force landed in February 1797. One writer has called this a comic opera invasion. That is how it might appear, when seen from a good space of time; it could easily have been a tragedy with great loss of life.

There have been many accounts, all differing slightly in details. The one full, documented, accurate story is in E. H. Stuart-Jones's book, *The Last Invasion of Britain*.

Briefly, and including the romantic red-petticoat story, the facts are that between 1,200 and 1,400 French soldiers, most of them released from prisons for the event, were landed under command of an American, General Tate. Their object was to cause confusion, to stir up strife and rebellion in England; and some of them genuinely believed an English Revolution, on the French pattern, was likely

* There are different spellings. This, the Ordnance version, is not correct Welsh! I am told it should be Preceli.

to break out with the least encouragement. They thought they could live off the country and were to have a free hand to pillage and collect booty enough to keep them for the rest of their lives.

The local forces, rather mixed—the Castlemartin Yeomanry, Fishguard Fencibles, local gentry, farmers, farm hands—were eventually organised by Lord Cawdor of Stackpole. He had less than 600. The French, instead of getting on with their invasion, were doing some petty looting, nothing terribly vicious; they seem to have been nervous, but there were a few casualties. And then they got the impression that Lord Cawdor had a strong force superior to their own.

Here is the petticoat story as written in 1880*.

An elderly lady deceased ten years ago, at the age of ninety, who was visiting Mrs. Ackland, and Captain, afterwards Colonel Ackland at Amroth Castle, when he left to meet the French, told me that a number of women, dressed in the Welsh costume, with scarlet cloaks, and their high-crowned black beaver hats, were made to go up a hill a moderate distance off, and to come out at some other point in such a way as appeared as if they were three times as numerous as they really were. One of the British officers directed the attention of the French to them, saying: "You see, we have abundance more troops." When the French laid down their arms these women came on the scene to show who they were, to the extreme wrath of the French.

The invasion had lasted two days!

Comic opera? Well, almost, perhaps. But it was a near thing.

Miss Curtis wrote "scarlet cloaks". I always was told *petticoats*— but perhaps a very lady-like Victorian woman would not say "petti-coat".

The women played all the best parts in the invasion. Jemima Nicholas finding some five Frenchmen looting took a pitchfork to them and they fled. Two Haverfordwest girls helped two prisoners to escape, steal a yacht and get back to France and there they married them. Everybody here was *very* angry, but when the girls and husbands came home on a visit years later all was forgotten and forgiven.

---

* *The Antiquities of Laugharne, Pendine and their Neighbourhood* by Mary Curtis.

# CHAPTER 5

# CARDIGAN TO BORTH

AT the mouth of the Teifi there is Cemmaes Head on the south and Cardigan Island on the north. This is a quiet spot a few miles from the busy little market-town, which in the past was important enough for a strong Norman castle, and was the scene of many a Norman-Welsh struggle. A very determined attempt was made by English kings to keep English influence supreme in these parts, perhaps because it could serve as a strongpoint for such a large area, also, I think because it could be reached by sea, thus saving those long forced marches through Welsh forests and over constantly rainy Welsh hills that Anglo-Norman soldiers hated so much. The effort to make Cardigan English is shown by the Charter of Richard II, which laid it down that only Englishmen should try and convict wrongdoers (as juries presumably) because of "the malice of the Welsh". The malicious Welsh rebelled often enough—successfully at times. The tradition of a Norman defeat in 1135 when 3,000 Normans were killed, has been mentioned in Chapter 3. Some were drowned when the bridge collapsed; indeed, so many were drowned that the living could cross the river by walking over the dead. Even the women—the Welsh ones—were taking prisoners. An old story, half true or quarter true. Today Cardiganshire is very Welsh indeed—Cardiganshire Welsh, which is not exactly the same thing as, say, Glamorganshire Welsh or Flintshire Welsh. But even the most extreme Welsh Nationalists would not throw you in the river. There is peace in the land.

Between Cardigan and the coast there is the lonely little village of Verwick (or Verwig), and then the land slopes down to the sea, and the precipitous Pembrokeshire cliffs give way to an entirely different coast scenery which runs almost the whole length of Cardigan Bay along both of the counties, Cardigan and Merioneth. This does not mean that there is no cliff scenery. There is, and in parts of south Cardiganshire the cliffs in some places are as tall and impressive as any you could find. In between are the coves, the sandy beaches,

the rock pools, the playgrounds for visitors and holiday makers.
The main road from Cardigan is good and often straight, but does
not follow the coast very closely. It is never far away, a couple of
miles at most, but the majority of visitors follow it then turn off to
their favourite village or beach, Aberporth perhaps, or Llangranog,
or New Quay, which is becoming so popular that if it gets many
more caravans it will have to put them on piles out in the bay to make
the old fishing village into a new Venice.

But if you go up the coast itself you see the structure changing;
from a few places you can see it from the road, but that is further
north, say at Aberaeron or Llanon. Briefly, though the land may
rise in cliffs, or in steep slopes, or sharply to the hilly hinterland of
the country, the foreshore widens.

Sometimes it is only the beach itself that is wider, sometimes
above the tides there is a bit of flat or gently sloping ground. There
is no uniformity. Some beaches are wide and not sandy at all, but
rock-strewn as far as you can see. Sometimes the land above high
water is rough and uncultivated, marshy or rushy, a home for
seaside flowers and the smaller seaside birds.

Now all this is explainable by a legend, but I have heard the
legend since I was a child and it is so clearly based on fact that I
seem to see the truth and not, as St. Paul said (of other things),
through a glass darkly.

Look westwards and Cardigan Bay lies before you. A very beautiful bay it is too. If you get up on a hilltop on a clear day you can see
the Merioneth hills dominated by Cader Idris, while further north
the Snowdon Range fades mistily into the peninsula of Lleyn. West
are the highlands of Central Wales; south, the miniature mountains
of Precelly. They say on a clear day you can see Ireland—would it
be the hills of Wicklow?—but I confess I have never seen them.
There are not all that many clear days here where the damp winds
of the Atlantic come blowing in. So to return to the first sentence
of this catalogue of beauties (to which I could add more for a long
time), Cardigan Bay is spread beneath your feet.

Once upon a time it was dry land.

First the legend.

The area where the bay is now was known as Cantref y Gwaelod,
the Lowland Hundred. It was low-lying and was protected from
flooding and inundation by walls and dykes. In one place there was
a great gate in the walls where flood water, during suitable tides,

could be allowed to flow out. Naturally it had to be closed most of the time. The gate was under the care of a man by the name Seithenyn. He was a heavy drinker and they called him Seithenyn the Drunkard. One day there was a great feast, and Seithenyn got drunker than ever before. He fell asleep, forgot the gates he had to close, and when the tide came in, it entered and flooded the country. This story is undoubtedly based on fact, though what all the facts are we shall never known. Some historians believe that this low-lying tract always was marshy and that it was the Romans who drained it and directed the first system of sea defences. It is certainly true that in at least three places up the coast there are causeways running out to sea. One is traceable westwards in the sea for twenty miles or so, and they all show evidence of having been erected by human hands. Some say no, these are natural reefs, perhaps boulder-covered in parts where tides have carried the stones. Surely both could be right, and whoever laboured on sea-walls and dykes used sarns (reefs) as their starting points and foundations. What convinced me was an old photograph taken far out in a shallow part of the bay in a very low tide. It showed the decayed stumps of a submerged forest.

If there was a forest there was land.

So going back to my starting point: the low, flat wide beach, which is a characteristic of so much of this bay, is a relic and reminder of when the Cardiganshire hills had miles of lowland lying between them and the sea.

Seithenyn the Drunkard, by the way, had a son by the name of Tudno. He became a priest (I *think* I have heard that this was an attempt at atonement for his father's sins), and going north he settled on a little island where he built a church. You can see the church today—or the one that was later erected on the spot—but the island has become part of the mainland and Llandudno (Tudno's Llan) has grown up around it.

Another story I heard is that up to about a hundred years ago this little church on the Great Orme was attached to Conway and that the curate of Conway rode out each Sunday to hold a service and that as a rule he had a congregation of one—his clerk.

Cardiganshire is full of preachers of all denominations. For years, as far back as I have been able to trace, a love of education has been like a flame burning over the hills of this county. At least from the beginning of the nineteenth century, Cardiganshire men, poor men, farmers, farm labourers, peasants have been struggling to educate themselves and pass on such knowledge as they pick up. Nowadays a school means an expensive building filled with expensive equipment; to them it was any building and teachers—houses were called academies, cottages were grammar schools, the meanest barn could be a place to learn your letters. At Tregaron the school was in the church at the foot of the church tower; every pupil brought peat for winter firing and the smoke used the tower as a chimney. I found an instance where children were taught in a barn—after the cows were turned out in the morning. Edward Richard of Ystrad Meurig closed his school for two years so that he could improve his own education. John Williams, one of his pupils, was, according to Sir Walter Scott, the finest schoolmaster in Europe.

These schools and these men were not merely teaching their pupils the alphabet and the rudiments of the three R's. They were giving a full classical education, the equal of any given at any public school in the country.

The curious fact is that when young men had acquired a good education they used it, nearly all of them, to become either teachers or clergymen of the Established Church or Nonconformist ministers. Seldom did they choose any other profession.

There was at that time hardly any drama in Wales; certainly none available to the poorer classes—the theatre, after the religious revival, became a place of sin and shame. So the drama moved to the pulpit. The focal point for religion was the sermon, and the sermon, whether the practitioners realised it or not, was often a dramatic exercise.

And so came the *hwyl*. This theatrical device consisted of the preacher working himself up into a frenzy and getting his congregation similarly moved. One of the greatest Welsh preachers in the early nineteenth century was Christmas Evans, born near the banks of the Teifi, first a farm labourer then an Anglesey minister, 'passing rich' (so they said) on £17 a year. He must (though he would hardly have known it) have been a born actor.

It was his tremendous passion, in conjunction with a peerless imagination that gave Christmas Evans so much power over a congregation. To see his huge frame quivering with emotion and to watch the lightning flash of his eye* . . . and to listen to the wild tone of his shrill voice . . . was to feel completely abandoned to the riotous enthusiasm of the moment. Abstractions, dry as the bones which Ezekiel saw of old in the valley he could clothe with

* He had only one eye.

sinews, flesh and skin and breathing life into them, make them stand on their feet.

That was the *hwyl*. A solo performance that could excite listeners to frenzy or have them cowering in their seats.

Now in this book I should not lead you far up the Teifi—not too far from the sound of the waves. But when storms threaten the seagulls go, so why should not we. Just this once!

At Cenarth you can see what may well be the last of a boat, the coracle, that has been in use for thousands of years. And near Llandussyl Caradoc Evans was born. Is he completely forgotten? "Caradoc Evans?" said a young man, a Cardie at that. "Who's he?"

Who *was* he? He died in 1945 and was buried on the Cardiganshire Hills above Aberystwyth. He was a Cardiganshire man who had a hard childhood and retained a little of its bitterness all through his life. He started work in drapers' shops, like an H. G. Wells or a Wellsian Kipps, and that did little to sweeten him. He escaped from the servile respectability of the draper's to become a journalist. He became a short-story writer, a novelist, a playwright and attacked his own people (his own relations, he said) with such virulence and at times with so much acid that for a while he must have been the most hated man in Wales. His play *Taffy* almost caused riots:

> My mind went back to the first performance of *Taffy*, for the production of it which Dennis Bradley paid, at a matinée at the Prince of Wales' Theatre. Welsh students in the gallery kicked up a row. Mrs. Lloyd George, who was in the audience, cried. Mrs. Asquith, as she then was, retained such memories of a Welshman who had dethroned her husband that she liked it.*

He saw the hypocrisy of zealous chapel people, their meannesses, their lies, their narrow-mindedness, and he opened these evils like sores and rubbed salt in the wounds.

And, all the time, he loved his Wales and his Welshmen. Loved them and winced when they lashed back at him.

He was a short-story writer of something near genius. Maybe he was a genius: it is a state I find difficult to describe and difficult to make up my mind about.

To me he was somewhat akin to Dylan Thomas. Only Dylan arrived in a more permissive and a more tolerant age. If Caradoc had written *Under Milk Wood* there would have been hysteria. They would have screamed for his head on a charger. I think he may have

* Hannen Swaffer.

written things as good: I am sure he wrote things (in another form) that were better.

He married, of all people, a romantic novelist, Countess Barcynska, or Oliver Sandys. No couple can ever have produced more dissimilar writing. But it was a successful marriage and, making allowance for such widely divided talents, a happy one. His widow's tribute to him, the biography, *Caradoc Evans* does not attempt to hide the flaws, yet is full of the love she had for this strange man. He came back to Cardiganshire, and in the end he was forgiven, and it was six strong Cardiganshire men who carried him to his grave facing Plynlimmon and Cader Idris and the Wales he loved, and it was a chapel minister who spoke the last words of eulogy at his funeral.

The finest preacher I ever heard in *hwyl* was the vicar of a parish in which I was the village schoolmaster. This is all called to mind by the Cardiganshire coast because the Reverend Edgar Evan Davies came from Aberaeron where his father was the doctor. The doctor had eleven sons, and they made up, and sometimes played as, a football team. Edgar Davies when I knew him had given up football as a worldly vanity. He was a good man who had become so strongly evangelical that almost everything that was worldly was suspect. No drinking, no smoking, no cards, no dancing, no radio. But when he preached he gave a performance for which lesser actors have been knighted. He could almost make your hair stand on end, but I am sure if anyone had suggested he was putting on a theatrical performance he would have been deeply shocked and grieved.

Oh, Cardiganshire was the place for *hwyl*.

It could be amusing too. An old friend called Tomos, which is enough name he thinks for me to use in telling a story against him, was a giant who was a horror on a Rugby field and a lamb off it. When the war finished he went to Aberystwyth College and trained as a teacher. He was grand with children and best of all with very young ones. On school practice he went once to a primary school, and when a lecturer visited him he had to tell a Scripture story as a demonstration lesson.

He chose the story of David and Goliath.

He told the story well, too. The shepherd boy taking delicacies to his soldier brothers, the tents, the armies that faced each other, swords being sharpened, the polish of armour, the raucous sneering defiance of the Philistine Giant, the despair of Saul and the Jewish captains.

And all the time Tomos was whipping himself up into excitement. His audience listened spellbound.

Then David saying *he* would fight the giant, the unbelief, the mockery, the final permission of King Saul, the trial of the king's armour and David's refusal to wear it.

Then David went forward to meet Goliath: the unarmed boy against the mighty giant.

By this time poor Tomos had worked himself into a fine state. As David he walked confidently; as Goliath he strode, he called his mocking cry, "Am I a dog . . . ."

The spear, thick as a weaver's beam was thrown, just missing the boy. Another spear from his armour bearer . . . .

Then David dipped his hand in his pouch, he selected one of the smooth stones he had chosen in the brook, fitted it in his sling . . . threw . . . .

"Whe — ee! *Smack*!"

Right in the middle of the great bully's forehead . . . . Tomos staggered . . . . even the visiting lecturer was fascinated . . . .

Tomos staggered . . . . Goliath staggered . . . .

Silence . . . .

Then up piped one small voice. "Please sir, did it hurt him?"

"Hurt him?" Tomos straightened himself. "HURT HIM? . . ." In a voice that could be heard from Cardiff Arms Park to Twickenham—"It bloody-well *killed* him!"

That is *hwyl*.

The west and the south-west gales batter the Cardiganshire coast hard at times. But not as roughly I think as they do north of the Bristol Channel. For one thing there is often that wide no-man's-land of foreshore to bear the brunt. Not many of the towns are so incautious as to push right out to the sea's edge. I have known Aberystwyth front to take some really heavy poundings now and again, but then, with respect, if you put your houses defiantly right up to the water some time or other the water will come right up to the houses. We found that out at Amroth. There was once a row of cottages—'The Cottages' they were called—on the south side of the lowest portion of the road. When the south-west winds *and* a high tide came together the cottagers put the furniture upstairs, barricaded the back doors—they faced seawards—and went to stay with relatives and friends. The sea took 'The Cottages' long ago, and the bakery stables for good measure.

On the whole the Cardiganshire folk are prudent. They do not, as Mrs. Parkinson did, sweep back the sea. They have had the sense to keep a respectful distance from it.

Another point about the storms in Cardigan Bay is that, as elsewhere, the prevailing wind is south-west. There are not a lot of good harbours up the bay, but there *are* a number of headlands jutting out to sea and, behind these, little bays facing north. Not too warm when a snow-cooled wind blows down from the Snowdon group, but quite good shelter in a south-westerly. There is a nice little open-to-north, quay-sheltered nook at New Quay; a harbour at Aberaeron; and another good one at Aberystwyth. This last visitors seldom see because it is at the wrong end of town for the holiday-makers, though in the early nineteenth century it thrived wonderfully on its 200 vessels and fluctuating body of about 800 seamen, which, for a quiet little place so far from any centre of population, was doing quite well. Most of the vessels took part only in coasting trade, but the county had prosperous lead mines and some silver, and no doubt that absorbed some of the shipping. You can see the remains of the lead mines almost anywhere by going a few miles inland; I understand that the silver was in the same ore.

There was a mint at Aberystwyth during the Civil War, and the land owners made fortunes. One Thomas Bushell gave Charles I a present of £40,000 and raised a regiment for him from the miners. Sir Hugh Myddleton, it is claimed, made some £25,000 a year from his mines. This might have been all very nice, but the money seldom stayed at home. Myddleton used his to give London its New River water supply. We can only hope that made the local miners happy. In fact, it did nothing of the sort. The miners were not well paid, while the water from the lead workings, under the influence of the acid from the hill peat bogs, was horrid stuff. About 1800 someone was writing, "It (mining) is a curse and not a blessing; the mines enrich a person or two in an age and entail poverty on hundreds for generations to come. The waters from the mines spread sterility over the adjoining fields, and kill all the fish in the rivers."

The lead-mines are silent now. Yet in 1900 there were still 900 miners in the country.

Most of the sheltered coves lie to the south of the country. From Aberaeron to Aberystwyth there is a fairly unbroken sweep, and what land runs seaward is too low to give shelter to a raft. The wreck

The River Teifi
Aberystwyth

(*Overleaf*)   Slate formation in the North Cardiganshire cliffs
Aberdovey

position was very bad. From 1743 to 1901 there were sixty-two reported wrecks. Goodness knows how many of small coastal craft or
fishing boats went unrecorded. The first lifeboat rescue we hear of
was when the Cardigan boat went to the rescue of the brig *Thetis* of
Newport and saved two lives. All the same, a seafaring tradition grew
up all along the coasts of this bay, and Cardiganshire and Merionethshire boys gravitated to a sailor's life like later ones everywhere wanted
to be engine drivers. Many of them remained seamen, but many
aimed higher, and to command a ship became a third local ambition
—after the Church and teaching. Here and there Schools began to
teach navigation. A lot of these local boys were content when they
got command of a coaster, but some went higher and became
captains and mates of vessels that went all over the world. Sailors
who could swear in Welsh could be met with in seaports anywhere
on the seven seas, and retired sea captains were as common in the
villages of the bay as blackberries in its hedges. It if comes to that
there still are a few.

Aberaeron is not an old town, as age goes in towns; up to about
1800 it was much less important than smaller, picturesque Aberarth
a mile to the north. Aberarth is marked on John Carey's map (1599),
but not Aberaeron. Then the jetties that give shelter to the harbour
were built, a coastal trade began, Aberaeron grew, and Aberarth
stayed as it was. The inland parts of the county are not too well
supplied with roads, even today: in the past parts of it were, for
trade purposes, almost inaccessible. So the coal, lime, timber and
slates brought into Aberaeron harbour were a useful addition to
the local economy, and I am told the boats took away corn and
miscellaneous farm produce. These, one assumes, they would take
to another port where there was a good market and roads rather than
hill tracks.

Everyone who knows Cardiganshire well knows of the two sides
of the county's sea tradition: the deep-water wanderings and the
coasting vessels. There was also some fishing, but not as a complete
way of earning a living except where the few good harbours were,
like the one at Aberystwyth. The small sailing coaster is as outdated
as the quinquereme, but what a boon it must have been when land
communications were bad.

Cardiganshire, away from its mild-climate seashore and fertile
lowland fields, goes almost unvisited though it is a fascinating,
picturesque and interesting part of the country. But communi-

The Dysynni River

(*Facing*) Dysynni Bridge, Merioneth
Dolgellau Bridge

G

cations can never have been good, and when wheeled vehicles became the means of transport, journeys over the hill roads must have
been dreadful. There was a beautiful Cistercian Abbey at Strata
Florida, and the ruins of it remain, but the people who visited it
would go on foot, as the monks of Abbey-cwm-hir in Radnorshire
did, or, the well-to-do, on horseback. Many did visit it; Strata
Florida was a famous meeting place for Welshmen, and a desirable
place, they considered, to be buried when they had finished with
earthly journeys. Westwards, on the seaward side, most of the roads
would have been tracks; eastwards most still are; and in winter the
Central Wales hills are inhospitable, lonely and cold in good
weather, impassable when it is bad.

There always have been markets at Tregaron, at Lampeter,
perhaps at one or two of the places in the Teifi valley, but in winter
none would be easy to reach from a distance. Between the hills and
the sea many people would find it easiest to go down the valleys to
some place like Aberaeron to sell their produce.

Inland I cannot see a lot of real change in recent years. A few
modern bungalows go up, a few caravans arrive, but the chapel is
still a power in the land, and the Sabbath is still a day when you
worship rather than play. It is only recently in the 1960s, that a
doctor friend, a great fishing enthusiast who had done good service
to a farmer's family, was told he must come and fish any of their
trout streams whenever he liked. He was worked harder than a
tinker's mule, but one day in the week he did try to keep a few
hours for himself.

"I'll be up one Sunday," he said.

"Nobody" said the farmer—he was speaking to a man to whom
he owed gratitude—"nobody fishes on my land on the Sabbath."

Another angler was refused permission to fish because he asked
in English. You or I might have been given it, but this man could
speak Welsh—and they knew it.

There is still some of the hard unbending character that Caradoc
Evans knew and pilloried in the Cardiganshire hills.

Chapel still rules, even if it is not quite as almighty as it was.
Young people are not as amenable to harsh discipline as their
parents were. The number of chapels at one time must have been
incredible: the numbers in the congregations I still find it hard to
swallow.

A Yorkshire writer by the name of J. Horsfall Turner wrote a book called *Wanderings in Cardiganshire* round about 1902 (it was undated). Apparently, judging by the dedication, his wife was a Cardiganshire woman, which would be why he wrote it, since all his other books were about Yorkshire. The book contains much of interest, but a disproportionate share is about ministers and parsons. There is an appendix listing the various nonconformist churches of the different denominations. Without making a complete count I made it roughly come to about 250. This, in a small isolated county; and the list does not include Church of England (as they were then, now Church of Wales). The congregations varied from thirty at Trichrug (which I've never heard of), to 1,150 at Tabernacle Aberystwyth, most being in the 250 to 500 range. At Lampeter in 1807 Owen Davies preached at a quarterly meeting to a congregation of 5,000.

I suppose the large families they had in the old days may have had something to do with these numbers, but, even so, a lot of people must have been very religious, or very afraid of being considered non-religious.

Along the coast things change more quickly, though it does not always follow that change is for the better. There are crowded caravan sites at many seaside villages. New Quay looks full to over-flowing; Borth at the north of the county also gets its share; and so does Aberystwyth, though they are tucked away behind the town. In fact, though the county is furthest from the modern Babels and has been 'discovered' much more slowly, it is getting yearly a larger share of visitors. The visitors are not as a rule inclined to share their hosts' religious observances, so you can recognise very easily anywhere the still sober Sabbath-observing Cardiganshire people on a Sunday, though, as already hinted, a lot of the young people have gone over to the enemy.

Not but what the devil needs to watch what he does in these parts. He came to put in his place a parson of Aberarth who had been insulting him rather too freely, but the parson fought back so persistently with bell, book and candle that the devil tried to escape by jumping from the tower. If you do not believe this you can go and see the marks he made with his hands and feet on the stone he landed on in the churchyard.

At Llanarth close by it is worth remembering that at The Wern, which was a country mansion then, Henry Tudor spent a night on his way from Milford to Bosworth, and there is a story that he found a lover there. She bore a son, and the descendants of this ap Harry (son of Harry), a branch of the Cardiganshire Parrys, were always afterwards conscious of and proud of their royal descent.

Llanon is a pleasant little village, narrow enough if you motor down the main road, but well spread out over the wide space between the village and the foreshore. The name comes from Non, and St. Non was the mother of St. David, the patron saint of Wales. All sorts of legends have grown up around his parentage and about his early life, and indeed about his whole life. The one thing that can be said with certainty is that some of the goodness and holiness of the man comes shining through the mists of time.

His father, it is said was Sand, or Sandde, who was descended from Cunedda, father of Ceredig, after whom the small princedom, Ceredigion (Cardigan) was named. He was born near St. David's (as it came to be called in his honour) at what is now called St. Non's chapel. His boyhood was spent at Llanon, and the story says he walked the six miles daily to school at Hen Fynyw (near Aberaeron). Later he was educated at Whitland Abbey (Carmarthenshire), where he was so modest that he did not even know what his teacher looked like because his head was always bowed humbly. His early life, after he became a priest (I am adding traditions together and writing them down as fact) was spent often in missionary journeys and in teaching the gospels. Where he preached and taught he established a *llan* (place) 'church' if you like, and there are more than fifty in Wales dedicated to him. He founded a monastery in the little hollow where St. David's Cathedral is today; he went to Jerusalem, where the Patriarch John III consecrated him; he brought back an altar stone which is still in his cathedral; he performed many miracles. He was:

> a mirror and a pattern to all, instructing both by word and example, excellent in his preaching, but still more so in his works. He was a doctrine to all, a guide to the religious, a life to the poor, a support to orphans, a protection to widows, a father to the fatherless, a rule to monks, and a model to teachers; becoming all to all, that so he might gain all to God.

To be a saint is it not necessary to be sometimes a sinner? Not a great sinner, look you, but just a small, small one so that the saint can understand sinners and love as well as chastise them.

I cannot find much wrong in St. David's behaviour at any time unless it was that unkindness to the nightingale.

St. David, as the tale goeth, being seriouse occupied in the night tyme in his divine orizons, was so troubled with the sweete tuninges of the nightingall, as that he cold not fasten his minde upon heavenlie cogitacions, as at other tymes, being letted by the melodie of the bird, praid unto th' almightie, that from that tyme forward, there might never a nightingall sing within his Dioces, and this saieth our weomen, was the cause of confininge of the bird out of this Countrey thus much to recreat the readers spirittes.*

R. M. Lockley† seemed to think the saint must have relented because a stray nightingale came to Pointz Castle in 1948, though no nest was found. I can go one better. When I was a nasty little nest-hunting boy (and that was a sad long time before 1948) I found a nest in the side of a grave in Amroth churchyard. The dark brown eggs—and I *did* know eggs quite thoroughly—I identified as those of the nightingale. I did not take even one egg though. There was a very strong local superstition that to take anything out of a church-yard was very unlucky—it *had* been known to cause death—and I knew better than to break rules of *that* sort!

When St. David's time came to die he was told by an angel what was to happen. The date was 1st March in the year 601, and he had reached the age of 147. He made all necessary preparations and the news spread.

Who then could endure the weeping and wailing of the people? the voice of the mourners was but one, for kings sorrowed for him as a judge, the old bewailed him as a brother, the young honoured him as a father, all revered him as they revered God. His body, carried in the arms of the holy brethren, was committed to the earth in his own city, but his soul is crowned for ever and ever.

The earliest inhabitants of Aberystwyth made their camps on the hill Pen Dinas, and I was about to add that they had more sense than settle where the alien sea could reach them and then I re-membered that in those days it is highly improbable that the sea came anywhere near. They settled on hill-tops, of course, because hill tops are more easy to defend than are the low places. Fishing seems to have been the earliest industry: it is recorded as early as 1206 "God gave an abnormal supply of fish". The castle was held for the King in the Civil War and was taken and put out of action as a fortress by Parliamentary troops. In 1740 there were thirty houses inside the town walls. No doubt there were more outside

* *Description of Pembrokeshire* by George Owen of Henllan (1603).
† *Pembrokeshire* (Regional Books) by R. M. Lockley (Robert Hale 1957).

them. In 1800 there were 500 houses and two good inns. The fishing gave way, as at Aberaeron to a coastal trade.

In 1860 came the notion that this place could become a holiday resort; a speculator offered a week's free holiday to anyone buying a return ticket from Euston, and he erected a hotel to cope with the rush. The rush did not come. In 1870 the derelict hotel was bought for about £10,000 and became the nucleus of Aberystwyth College. And where more fitting than education-hungry Cardiganshire to start the Welsh university dreamed of by Owain Glyndwr many centuries earlier? The Cardiganshire spirit showed itself again when money ran short. Many well-to-do Welshmen did their share, but it was from the money contributed by the poor that Aberystwyth really rose from its first year's twenty-six students to its present status.

In the end the town got its seaside resort status, but people found their way unbidden and without being bribed to come.

A stone's throw inland (I mean an Arthur's stones throw; he threw boulders tons in weight as easily as David the shepherd boy threw pebbles) is the ancient church of Llanbadarn-fawr. (There is another place in Radnorshire with the same name.) Here, some say, was born Dafydd ap Gwylim, the greatest lyric poet Wales ever had. But another account says he was born in Glamorganshire. He was buried (another tradition, but a moderately likely one) at Strata Florida Abbey. In between there was much poetry and much love: which inspired which is not clear.

A few miles north, the great marsh of Cors Fochno between the Borth foreshore and the Dovey and the foothills is associated with Taliesin, bard, mystic and perhaps a greater poet than the better-known Dafydd.

Of him there are so many legends and folk tales that it is difficult to weld them into one coherent account. The one I like best is how, after several changes he was a grain of wheat whereupon the witch Ceridwen turned herself into a black hen and swallowed him.

> Then was I for nine months
> In the womb of the hag Ceridwen.

When he was born he was so beautiful—Taliesin, the Radiant Brow—that she let him live.

He became chief bard to King Arthur, then to King Urien. I do not know how his poetry survived nor who made the English versions, but some of it is nearly obscure enough to be twentieth-century respectable.

> I was with my lord in the highest sphere
> On the fall of Lucifer into the depths of hell;
> I have borne a banner before Alexander;
> I know the names of the stars north and south;
> I was in Canaan when Absolom was slain . . .

And so on. He instructed Eli. He was at the Crucifixion. He was with Noah and stood by the manger of the ass. He companied Moses and Mary Magdalene.

> I shall be until the day of doom on the face of the earth;
> And it is not known whether my body is flesh or fish.
> · · · ·

And at length I am Taliesin.

Scholars have written volumes about him; how can I expect to explain (what anyhow I do not know) him and his poetry in a page? He was buried at Bedd Taliesin.

After Aberystwyth there are cliffs of slate, or so they look to me, and there are slate pavements in some of the quietest streets in the town, and many old houses have slate floors. There is a cove or two; many holiday makers find these more to their taste than the formal resort; and tucked-away Clarach is fast becoming popular. Borth was a village, but year by year it grows. The sands, however, stretch for a few miles, out beyond Borth and fronting the sand-dunes. Then there is the Dovey and by road it is a mighty long trek to the village-town of Aberdovey just across the estuary, for you must go the miles up to Machynlleth and down again the other side. But the beach on the south of the estuary is a pleasant spot to linger. I do not know the first thing about conchology—which is merely an ugly way of saying, the study of shells—but you can pick up unusual and very pretty ones high on the beach here, while down in the shallow water at low tide the smaller water birds—the dunlins, the sandpipers, Mother Carey's chickens, and all the rest—go about their lawful business finding their food in the rocky pools.

# CHAPTER 6

# THE COAST OF MERIONETH

BELOW Machynlleth Bridge the Dovey soon opens out into its estuary and it is hard to decide where river ends and estuary begins. At low tide the sands stretch in all directions, clean too, for the Dovey comes swiftly down from the rock-hard hills of Merioneth-shire, and mud is the least of their exports. Those sands though, I do not trust them. I like my sands stone-hard where the tide comes and goes at a sedate pace, where there are no unknown deeps, no unexpected shallows; no channels and no sandbanks. Not that I remember hearing of anyone being tricked in the Dovey before it reaches the sea, but where there are miles of sand the incoming tide is nearly always in a hurry.

When you get down stream to Aberdovey you are back almost where you started on the beach at Borth, but this is lovely country, hilly above the river bank, wooded and never harshly precipitous; to go up river to Machynlleth Bridge and down again is no hardship.

I read somewhere an old account of Aberdovey in which it said there were only three houses, but no date was given, so it must refer to a very long time ago, for it is included in a 1565 return of "Havens and Creeks of the County of Merionethshire". According to an 1801 return (I am sorry to leap so abruptly across the centuries) there were only two ports in the county, Barmouth being the other. In a way the pattern of coast begun in Cardiganshire is continuing. The shore, being the land that once lay above Cantref y Gwaelod, is also similar, the hills lying close to a wide foreshore that may be cultivated but often is not. Below this there are rocky pools or sands. The pattern is repeated, yes; yet there is a subtle difference, and I am not quite sure what it is. I do not think there are quite as many little capes giving shelter from the southwest, so perhaps this part seems a little more stormy, a little more wind-beaten, and while the same sea-going tradition exists I think, in a broad general way, Cardiganshire produced most sailors and Merioneth most ships. Aberdovy was once a headquarters for the herring fleet of the bay—

that is in the season, for they were not always present—and you can hear of thirty herring boats at a time waiting for a tide. Thirty good herring boats would have made the harbour quite lively. I don't know if the herrings stopped coming, but they helped the little Aberdovey of those days to grow prosperous. The French boats came too, though whether there was a fishing limit in those days I was not told.

Ship-building was carried on at Aberdovey and Barmouth during the nineteenth century. Probably earlier, but there are few records available, though I have read that it was done in all the creeks along the coast. That would hardly give the two main centres much competition for there are not enough deep-water creeks to count. There still exist particulars of some of the work done. For instance a sea-going boat would take a year to build. Prices, which must surely have varied, were between £2 and £3 a ton. A schooner of 292 tons built in 1879 cost forty-five shillings a ton. The total bill was £543, and there was a curious item, £2, travelling expenses, though who travelled and where is not mentioned. It was, however, hardly a charge to quarrel with even then when a man could go a lot further for a lot less money than he could today.

A steamship was built in 1854. It was called the *Mountain Maid*, so probably was for a local buyer. The last from the Aberdovey shipyards was the *Olive Branch* in 1880, but I have a feeling that small open fishing craft may have been made later. The *Twelve Apostles* was built at Aberdovey in 1858. She was wrecked at Hell's Mouth, Porth Nigel (Caernarvonshire) in 1898, and when they rang the Lutine Bell at Lloyds the announcement was made that "*The Twelve Apostles* have been found in Hell's Mouth". The story is told that, when she was driven in, two doves came and alighted on the mast. It may be a coincidence, but no lives were lost in this wreck.

"Of course," said the person who told me, "sailors are awful superstitious, man."

And landsmen are not!

The Fishguard Invasion, though many people outside Wales know little about it, is fairly well documented, and anyone who wants to can find out the facts. An earlier invasion on Cardigan Bay is almost completely obscured by time and lack of verifiable facts. It is not even known for certain where it took place, but Aberdovey seems to be the most likely spot. It was a fairly small, almost homely invasion, mind. What happened was that in 1597 a Spanish ship landed, apparently in search of food. A number of houses (farms perhaps; there were not many Aberdovey houses then) were raided, and by all accounts the food—which may have been animals—was siezed. Then some of the county forces, a sort of militia, appeared and killed two of the invaders. The rest returned to their ship, but the defenders sniped at them and picked off four more. After that the Spaniards sailed away.

It is a slight story but at the time it must have been rather more than a nine-days wonder locally.

The county has usually had a small military force of some kind. I believe private armies became illegal, though my history has grown so weak I can neither remember nor discover when. But I am almost sure that Captain Corbett, who marched the Towyn volunteers south to help repel the French at Fishguard, paid the expenses of this local regiment, if that is not too grand a word, out of his own pocket. There certainly was a Merionethshire militia soon after this time, because it is on record that they were stationed at Deal during the Napoleonic invasion scare.

And a high old time they must have had! They were allowed to have their wives with them—but only "*some*" took advantage of that privilege! Discipline was easy, and a favourite sport was stealing local poultry. Apparently the commander-in-chief issued an order deprecating this little pastime. It seems as if authority could be tough at times, for at a garrison court martial at Sandwich one William Williams was sentenced to 300 lashes for stealing a pair of shoes.

I understand that these sentences were seldom carried out in full and could be remitted altogether, though in the navy one gets the impression that conditions were brutal at times.

But naval crews were often hard customers. Many were 'pressed' men, and there are accounts of the press gang at work on this coast, even up as far as Dolgelly; and when they were known to be in the neighbourhood suitable men made themselves scarce and hid until the danger had passed.

On the south Gower coast certain of the caves are still pointed out as those in which the local young men hid themselves when the press gang was around.

An 1803 order from the War Office was that news of an invasion was to be signalled by hill-top beacons. The Lord Lieutenant of

Merionethshire pointed out to their lordships that it was not feasible in this county. There were too many hill tops. It is not recorded whether or when the War Office cancelled their instructions, but as long as they were in force a number of local men must have done very well for themselves. There were four to a beacon, and each man had three shillings a day. Not bad money in those times for doing nothing!

From Aberdovey to Barmouth the coast makes a wide curve out to sea and then in again, with the two wide estuaries of the Dovey and the Mawddach at its south and north. Inland the hills rise, range on range grouped round Cader Idris, the Chair of Idris. To spend a night in the Chair is to take a risk, for if you do so the morning will see you a poet or a madman. The superstition does not relate this, but there have been men who were both. Anyhow it is a lovely mountain to look on from the country around, and though it must be treated with respect—all the Welsh hills should be—I have the feeling that it is not as inhospitable as loftier Snowdon. At any rate I don't seem to hear of so many accidents on its slopes; perhaps fewer people climb it.

The only place of any size on this bit of coast is Towyn, though there are plenty of pleasant villages both by the coast, and inland. The district around has been used by the army as a training ground for some years, but the army comes and goes like men in Tennyson's *Brook*; but Towyn seems to follow the example of that stream itself by "going on for ever". It certainly was there a very long time ago for in the church you can see the (presumed) seventh-century stone, St. Cadvan's stone, with an inscription on it that some scholars claim is the earliest written Welsh in existence. Other scholars say it is not. One of them even translated it—upon which another said the translation was completely inaccurate. I suppose this arguing passed the time for them.

About the accounts for the town's stocks and whipping post made in 1757 there can be no argument. They cost £1 9s. 1d. exactly ("That's right, to the ha'penny", as one local farmer said when he worked out by his ready reckoner that twenty ewes at £1 each came to £20).

The wood in the stocks was the most expensive item:

| | |
|---|---|
| To Timber | 13s 6d |
| To carr ditto | 1s 3d |

| To iron and making by the smith | 5s |
| To two locks | 1s 8d |
| To tarr | 8d |
| To a Constable Staff | 1s |
| To my work in making the Stocks and Whipping Post | 6s |
| | £1  9s  1d |

Apparently towns could be fined by the quarter sessions if they did not provide these instruments of punishment.

North of Towyn the Dysynni River comes down from Cader Idris and Tal-y-llyn lake, opening out into a sort of lagoon, Broad Water, north of Towyn. Between Towyn and Tal-y-llyn there is still the narrow-gauge railway, though only the enthusiasm of private individuals has saved it from closure.

The 1565 returns of Havens and Creeks listed Barmouth as having four houses and two small boats used as ferries. There could not have been much travelling then, and two ferries to four houses seems disproportionate. But probably the survey was made by someone who did not understand the district. The Welsh taste always did run to isolated dwellings rather than built-up towns and no doubt there were plenty of houses scattered around. Thomas Pennant, gentleman, naturalist, topographer and gossip, when he paid a visit about 1777 found a sizeable town. Barmouth Bridge was built in 1867, and since they reserved a width of it for a footbridge that would have made the ferries redundant. Barmouth shared the Merioneth shipbuilding with Aberdovey.

An engraving of Barmouth Harbour made in 1829 shows a boat in course of building.

There are in existence some of the bills for ship building at Barmouth. The sloop *Unity* was built for C. Rees Edwards and contained some very unusual items:

| Main sail | £16 18s 4¼d |
| Pepper | ½d |
| Speaking trumpet | 2s |
| Mouse trap | 1s |
| North Sea chart | 15s |

It would have been a pity to leave that farthing off the cost of the sail. And who wanted a ha'pennyworth of pepper and a mousetrap?

Apparently the *Unity* was used to trade with Danzig. Danish dues were at that time payable at Elsinore, first so much per ship and then by tonnage. They were abolished in 1857, and, the *Unity* being the last to pay them, the Danes gave souvenir bowls with the ship and her name painted on them. I was told there were still a few of these bowls in existence here and there, but I have never seen them, though it seems somebody once showed me a picture of one.

When Thomas Pennant was at Barmouth during his tour of Wales (about 1777) he did not mention ship building, but he did have a little to say of the coastal trade.

> I found the little town of Barmouth, seated near the bottom of some mountains, and the houses placed on the steep sides, one above the other, in such a manner as to give the upper an opportunity of seeing down the chimneys of their next subjacent neighbours. The town is seated very near to the sea, at the mouth of the river Maw, or Mawddach; and takes its name of Barmouth, i.e. Aber Maw, or Mawddach from that circumstance. At high water, the tide forms here a bay, about a mile over, but the entrance hazardous, on account of the many sandbanks. This is the port of Merioneddshire; but not so much frequented as it ought to be, because the inhabitants do not attempt commerce on a large scale, but vend their manufactures through the means of factors, who run away with so much of the advantages which the natives might enjoy; yet ships now and then come to fetch the webs or flannels; and I am informed that a few years ago, forty thousand pounds worth have been exported in a year, and ten thousand pounds worth of stockings. Many of the webs are sold to Spain and from thence sent to South America.

I think Pennant was more fascinated by a fasting woman who lived at Barmouth than by its trade. Her name was Mary Thomas; he paid her a visit, and, though *most* phenomenal fasts have been based on fraud, he seems to have been convinced hers was genuine: "She is deprived of the use of her lower extremeties, and quite bed ridden, her pulse rather strong, her intellects clear and sensible". She was 47 then and had been an invalid for twenty years, the first few of which she had been in a coma. Her diet was a morsel of bread (seven grains) and a wineglass of water or wine a day. She was still alive in 1809 when she was 85 years old, and she always remembered Pennant's visit.

The coast at Barmouth runs in a wide estuary nearly up to Dolgellau. The river is the Mawddach, and the scenery here, with the wide arm of water and thickly wooded hills with their background of mountains, must be about the loveliest in Wales. They claim hereabouts that there is only one view in the world better than looking down the Mawddach, and that is the view looking up. Dolgellau is above the navigable part of the river, but there are grounds for believing that ages ago the sea came further inland than it does now. The chief evidence lies in Harlech, a little way up the coast. Now between Harlech Castle and the sea is Morfa Harlech, a wide waste of low land and a ridge of sand dunes. Yet it is said that when the castle was built, and for ages afterwards, the sea came to the foot of the rocks on which the castle stands. Another significant fact is that there is not far from the town the Cistercian Cymmer Abbey, which had some sort of sea trade. One of its fields is Cae y Llong (the Field of the Ship), and another was Cae y Stabal, a staple being wool baled ready for shipment. Another interesting fact is that by the charter of the abbey its ships were free of tolls.

Pennant relates that he saw a sloop ready for launching at Llanelltyd and that is only about a mile below Dolgellau.

Dolgellau lying snugly under Cader Idris is a fine strong town and all the older houses are built of heavy dark stone that can look very sombre in dull weather but very pleasant when the sun shines. A lot of these old houses are paved with slate, and one I have been in had slate stairs and slate bannisters to them. I have always thought that buildings with unhappy associations were in some way unpleasant in atmosphere, yet one day I was having tea in Dolgellau and remarked to one of the staff what a pleasant, well-proportioned room it was, and how light and airy, and she said yes, it was once the town gaol. It had been, too, and outside they have propped up the old gaol door studded and as strong as the door of Ali Baba's cave. So away flies one of my most cherished superstitions. But perhaps they were not unkind to their prisoners in Dolgellau; perhaps they had no wrongdoers, and the gaol never was used. Or perhaps it was like the gaol I saw in Andorra in the Pyrenees. As long as they could remember it had had only one occupant, and he went out to the local wine-shop each evening to drink with his friends. He got into the habit of staying out so late that they threatened to lock him out altogether unless he came back in decent time.

The Welsh gold mines are not far from Dolgellau and, though I do not think any are worked at the moment, they could be; that is they have not been allowed to become derelict. I am no expert on gold-mining but I have been assured there is plenty of gold still in

the hills, but that it costs more than its value to extract it. I peered
into the river bed once to see if I could spot just one tiny nugget for
a souvenir, but somehow gold never finds its magnet in me.

As for the wool trade Pennant noted in Barmouth, you can still
buy a bit of good home-woven Welsh flannel, or wool, in Dolgellau,
and in the eighteenth century the town was the centre of the trade.
The value of flannel woven in farms and cottages round about 1800
was some £100,000 a year. Another local trade was in woollen
knitted stockings, and this also was very profitable. The local women
in most of Central Wales knitted in *all* their spare time, even while
walking to and coming from market, and I remember when I was
quite young an old Merionethshire woman telling me they were still
knitting when she was a girl. I particularly remember that because
she had been a maid on a farm, and they were allowed candles or
rushlights to knit by. But when the moon shone brightly all lights
were put out and they had to sit on the window seat and knit by
moonlight. I do not think that was exactly meanness, but, my word,
it was the most extreme frugality. When she told me I don't think
I knew exactly what a rushlight was, but one day a Welsh farmer
friend made me some, and at a sale I was able to buy a rushlight
holder in which to burn them.

William Cobbett gives instructions on how to make these tiny
lights in *Cottage Economy*, and he was full of praise for them:

> I was bred and brought up mostly by rushlight, and I do not find that I see
> less clearly than other people. Candles certainly were not much used in
> English labourers' dwellings in the days when they had meat dinners and
> Sunday coats. Potatoes and taxed candles seem to have grown into fashion
> together; and, perhaps, for this reason: that when the pot ceased to afford
> *grease* for the rushes, the potatoe-gorger was compelled to go to the chandler's
> shop for light to swallow the potatoes by, else he might have devoured peeling
> and all!

There is not much left of Cymmer Abbey, but enough is left,
as with many Cistercian buildings, to show what a grand place it
must have been. It is often believed that this order always chose
places of great natural beauty for their abbeys. That is not quite
correct. The rule was that they had to choose the quietest, the most
lonely places. And so often those are places of natural beauty. They
were great farmers, and they cultivated, bred their flocks and herds,
cleared streams, planted woods. Where they let land to tenant
farmers they were excellent landlords. The strange thing is that all

their houses fell into ruin, and the stone from the ruins found its way into so many local new buildings. Generally speaking, as at Tintern, and Vale Crucis, much was left, but in other places the stones were taken, as at Abbey-cwm-hir, until hardly anything was left at all. Since for a long time the Welsh clung to the old religion, and since, as a rule, the people in these quiet places were very superstitious, I find it strange that they raided what to them must still have been holy places. Perhaps it was the unsuperstitious who pulled down their barns and built greater.

There is gold in the hills, and there is treasure in the hills also. Buried treasure is, of course, fairy tale material and romantic—and generally non-existent outside the imagination. But sometimes it has been discovered. There may still be a little left here and there. Quite a lot of money was dug up at one time and another at Kent-chester, the Roman town near Hereford, and 18,000 gold coins were found in three jars near Kerne Bridge in the lower Wye valley. I *think* if I had been the abbot of a monastery and had had some treasure in my care I would have liked to keep at least a little out of the hands of Master Thomas Cromwell's servants. After all, many monks must have thought that some day the bad times would come to an end and they would return. I do not think that anything they hid could now come to light except by chance, but strange things do happen.

On 13th February 1890 two men were prospecting for gold in the neighbourhood of the ruins of Cymmer Abbey. When they were excavating they dug up two metal objects in very bad condition. They were neither excited, nor specially pleased but they cleaned them up a bit—one was a cup, one was a plate—and sold them for fifty shillings. Quite a useful little sum for those days for a dirty old plate and cup.

Their employer was a man by the name of Roberts. He heard of what had happened and said that these objects really belonged to him. He got them back, but there is no record of whether he paid the fifty shillings. Let's hope the finders had spent theirs, anyhow.

Roberts must have had an idea that these were no ordinary old utensils, for he had them cleaned, and it turned out that they were a silver gilt chalice and paten. It was assumed (I have never heard if there was any actual proof) that they had belonged to Cymmer Abbey.

The full particulars are that these were two perfect examples of

Dolgellau
Merioneth Beach

late thirteenth-century church plate. They were made in Herford in Westphalia. The Chalice was 7¾ inches high, with a bowl 7⁵⁄₁₆ inches in diameter and 2 inches deep. The Paten was 7⁵⁄₁₆ inches in diameter. The total weight was 46 ounces.

The news got around, and in 1892 the crown put in a claim for the two pieces on the ground that they were treasure trove. They were a bit late. The treasure had long since been sold by Christies. A merchant named Boone from the Strand had bought the two for £710 and had sold them to Baron Schoeder for £3,000.

Check, if not check-mate! Mr. Roberts did not seem to have much trouble getting a grubby old plate and cup from his employees and neighbours. Baron Schoeder was another matter. You didn't knock on his door and say you wanted that cup and plate back, please!

What did happen I cannot say exactly but I understand there was a gentleman's agreement about it all. This became evident when Schoeder died for he left the cup and dish to King George V. King George handed them over to the National Museum of Wales.

I still hope those two unnamed chaps kept their fifty bob. But telling their story here and there must have earned them free drinks for quite a while, anyhow.

Another thought is what else did the monks tuck away to wait for the day of their return.

Treasure of another kind. In the early 1800s the Portuguese boat *Carminhando* was wrecked near Barmouth with the loss of all hands. The cargo was worth £6,000. It consisted of ninety-six pipes of wine. (Shades of *Whisky Galore*, and my Daddy and Shellard and McGuire boring with their gimlet into a barrel of lard!) Anything might have happened, but a body of Barmouth men were recruited and guarded the wine until it could be handed over to whoever it rightfully belonged to.

This sober behaviour would certainly not have happened in some places on the coast. The Barmouth men must have been a very honest, God-fearing lot. Or did they have a gimlet?

The road runs north from Barmouth through a lot of villages and past one of the most magnificent castles in the country. That, of course is Harlech. The road continues, crosses Traeth Bach to Penrhyndeudraith, then over the dyke or dam Maddocks made to drain the marshy ground in the lower basin of the River Glaslyn; and so on to Portmadoc, by which time we are in Caernarvonshire.

Harlech Castle

H

All the way up this road the mountains rise magnificently to the east, while on the west is Cardigan Bay. Between road and sea are two roughly triangular stretches of flat land. The first is called Morfa Dyffryn, the one north of Harlech is called Morfa Harlech. *Mor* is sea; *Morfa* is, roughly, beach, or, more properly, a wide foreshore. (I don't think it translates *exactly* into English.)

It seems strange that south in this bay the sea has advanced and submerged the land, while in the north there are these large tracts where the sea has had to retreat. They *are* large tracts, but when you study them on the map they are not as large as all that, not compared with the bay as a whole. My own belief is that land was submerged in the whole of Cardigan Bay, but currents, *and* strong south-west winds and moveable deposits from what went under the water further south, were brought up north. It must have been a long time ago, and it must have taken place very slowly, but the land took back a little from the sea. If you look carefully on a map you can almost *see* these two beaches rising as tide and currents laid them down. The tips of Morfa Dyffryn and Harlech Point like two snub noses are most significant. They are not so very high above sea-level at that, but near the sea's edge sand-dunes have in places put up protective barriers as if to guard the levels behind. Most of the area has little recorded history, but the tradition of the sea coming to the foot of the rocky base of Harlech castle is met time and time again.

The foreshores are cultivated in places; near the sea they are often made up of sand dunes; while in some places they are, at best, only very rough pasturage. In quite a lot of places they are used as caravan sites. These sites are both popular and populous. Some look as though not one more caravan could be squeezed in. I don't know what would happen if they built a motorway right through Wales from east to west. At the moment the position is akin to, if not exactly the same as when English armies came on their periodic invasions: and that is, there is not a really good wide road through the mountains. Without going into route details too deeply, the visitor can come along the A5 in the north, or down through Bala to Dolgellau, or up from Central Wales again through Dolgellau. Whichever road is used, there are some precipitous hills—not that the modern car cannot tow a caravan up them, but they do look formidable at times—or the roads are twisting and narrow; and sometimes they are hilly *and* twisting and narrow.

The hinterland—I wish there were a good English or Welsh word for that—of mountain that guards the coast here rises to two heights, a little over 2,000 feet, called the Rhinogs, Rhinog Fach and Rhinog Fawr. These fall on the east to a fairly straight south-north road from Llanelltyd (near Dolgellau) to Maentwrog at the head of the estuary called Traeth Bach. Now this hinterland is mainly mountain and moorland and small hill farms. It is walkers' country, with streams and lakes—and a few nasty bogs—plenty of fresh air, mountain birds, and some of the finest scenery as you look north to the Snowdon range as you are likely to see anywhere. West is the Irish Sea and southwards Cader Idris; on a clear day you would hardly know which way to look, so fine is the scenery. On a misty day, now that is another matter; but far better not to get caught here when the mists come down. There may be hamlets somewhere, but they are small and few and far between.

This district is of great interest to the archaeologist and historian who (if he's the same man) knows what he is about and what he is looking for. There are standing stones and ancient encampments and cromlechs. Pennant said there were many traces of the Roman occupation in the area. It seems probable the famous south-north Roman road known as Sarn Helen because it was named in honour of Helen, wife of the Emperor Maximus, was what is now the Dolgellau-Maentwrog road or ran very near it. But Sarn Helen is difficult to trace, and the name crops up more frequently than does the ancient highway itself. More in evidence are the Roman Steps, a kind of paved highway through the mountains. They too are something of a mystery, and nobody can say for certain what they are or who made them. Some experts say they were meant to link up a westerly settlement with Sarn Helen; others are sure that it was a way by which the ancient Britons carried the minerals—gold, perhaps lead—that the Romans mined in this area. Or they could have been for pack animals.

As a rule I like my antiquities not too far from the main road these days. Arthur's Quoit, not far from Dyffryn, is worth a trek though, and it can be reached by going up a hill to the fine old Elizabethan house called Cors-y-gedol, which, like a lot of other houses in North Wales, has been put to the credit of Inigo Jones. But the house was built in 1592, and Inigo was only 20 then so we won't go into that too closely. The cromlech is in a field not far from the house. There are stones all over Wales that Arthur threw for one reason or another. He evidently was not warned 'Don't throw stones', as we were repeatedly. And look how famous it has made him. As far as we know the cromlechs were burial places, and no doubt the people of those days had quite simple techniques for getting those massive rocks into place. Most experts say that when the chamber was completed and the burial rites over, the whole would be covered with soil, but when you look at them as they are today, they look formidably heavy and a little grim. A few are in out-of-the-way places, but this particular Merionethshire example must have been sited by someone with an eye for a view.

Menhirs, or standing stones, are another feature that have not been explained to everyone's satisfaction. Various reasons have been offered, and it has occurred to me that more than one may be correct. They could be memorials *and* places of worship *and* mark the line of a route . . . and so on. There are two standing in a field near the village of Llanbedr, one tall, the other short.

Close to Llanbedr the sea becomes a kind of lagoon, a mile or two long, with a narrow spit of land between it and the sea. This is Mochras or Shell Island (I don't think it ever is an island these days) noted for the number and variety of shells on its shores. At Llanfair is buried Ellis Wynne, a Welsh poet who wrote an allegory *Bardd Cwsg*, the Sleeping Bard, which was published in 1703. This is quite a landmark in Welsh literature because it is a fine example of pure idiomatic Welsh and also gives a good picture of his times.

I like the little villages of the north Merioneth coast, but they are all over-shadowed by the significence of Harlech Castle. There were only two great Norman fortresses in the county; the other, Bere Castle is almost a complete ruin. Harlech is, or looks, as grand as it must have been in 1283 when it was completed.

It is nearly certain that there was some sort of castle here from the earliest times. In the *Mabinogion* it was Twr Branwen, the Tower of Branwen. She was Branwen of the White Neck, a lovely title for a lovely woman. She was one of the three most beautiful women in Wales and sister to Bran, King of all Britain. Alas, beauty does not mean happiness, and, though she married a king of Ireland, hers was a sad story, and she returned in sorrow to Wales to die in Anglesey.

Harlech Castle features much in history. It was often besieged but seldom taken. Owain Glyndwr did capture it, though only after a hard struggle. That was about 1404. Margaret of Anjou, wife of

Henry VI, came for refuge after the Battle of Northampton in 1460.

The best story is of the defence in the Wars of the Roses by that fine old warrior, Dafydd ap Jevan ap Einon. The attacking forces were led by Sir Richard Herbert, brother of the Earl of Pembroke. Defending castles was not a new experience for Dafydd. "I have held a castle in France till all the old women in Wales heard of it," he said. "Now I will hold a castle in Wales till all the old women in France hear of it."

A gallant boast, but in the end he was starved out. Sir Richard offered him honourable terms. Edward IV was not willing for this, but Sir Richard was as brave as his adversary had been.

"If you do not agree, sire, I will leave Dafydd where he is," he stated, "and you may send whom you like to get him out for I will not do it."

Edward gave in, and Dafydd and his hungry followers came out with colours flying and playing (on what instrument I cannot guess) that stirring tune "The March of the Men of Harlech".

In the Civil War the castle was at different times held by both sides, and in the end was the last castle in North Wales to hold out for the King. There does not seem to be a record of any thorough 'slighting' or making useless as a fortress, that happened to so many castles, so it may have remained in fairly good shape, though no doubt much has been done since to keep it so. We all pay lip service so readily to noble sentiments that it is pleasant to record that here one has actually been proved true. For Harlech Castle the pen has been mightier than the sword. It is the headquarters of 'Coleg Harlech', an educational experiment that long ago grew out of its experimental stage so that Harlech has become a most important centre of adult education in Wales.

What, I wonder, was the "mephetic vapour" which, Pennant said, troubled Morfa Harlech in 1694.

A mephetes, or pestilential vapour, resembling a weak blue flame, arose, during a fortnight or three weeks, out of a sandy marshy tract, called Morfa Bychan, and crossed over a channel of eight miles to Harlech. It set fire on that side to sixteen ricks of hay and two barns, one filled with hay, the other with corn. It infected the grass in such a manner, that numbers of cattle, horses, sheep and goats, died; yet men went into the midst of it with impunity. It was easily dispelled; any great noise, such as the sounding of horns, the discharging of guns, or the like at once repelled it. It moved only by night; and appeared at times, but less frequently, the following summer; after which this phaenomenon ceased.

North of Morfa Harlech is Traith Bach, where the River Dwyryd comes down from the lovely Vale of Ffestiniog, and the not-so-pretty slate quarries. There is a causeway over the estuary here and on its northern bank is Portmeirion, the Italian-style village designed by Mr. Clough Williams-Ellis. Then comes Traeth Mawr, which was once "a large extent of sands between the counties of Caernarvon and Meinonedd, of most dangrous passage to strangers, by reason of the tides which flow here with great rapidity".

# CHAPTER 7

# THE ROAD ROUND LLEYN

THE Gwynant and the Glaslyn come down from the Snowdon group of mountains and meet at Aberglaslyn. The pass here is one of the beauty spots of Wales, with precipitous hills high on each side and the rivers between tumbling each in a boulder-strewn bed. Once this really was the *aber* or mouth of the Glaslyn, and there was enough water below to allow small ships to come up to it. South of it the wide marsh estuary was and is known as Traeth Mawr.

More than one man saw the possibility on an embankment across this tract. Once the tide was dammed back, drainage could reclaim a large area of rich land from the marshes. Sir John Wynn of Gwydir was thinking about the scheme in 1625, but he had neither the engineering ability nor the knowledge to be able to do anything about it. "My skill is little and my experience none in these matters." He tried to get Sir Hugh Myddleton interested. Myddleton had worked out a scheme for supplying London with water and knew how such things could be done. Sir John tried a Scripture text: "We have heard of thy great workes done abroad, doe somewhat in thine own country."

But Sir Hugh was not interested. He replied that the work would be too expensive; he was too busy; he was too old; and—he too sounded as if he knew the Scriptures—"My wieff being also here, I cannot leave her in a strange place." It was near enough to "I have married a wife and therefore cannot come."

It was in 1798 before anything was done. In that year William Alexander Maddocks, Member of Parliament for Boston, bought an estate at Tremadoc and made plans for the embankment that had been visualised (if we accept that Wynn of Gwydir was not the first to think of it) centuries before.

By 1810 the work was under construction, but there were many setbacks. A storm in 1812 nearly destroyed what had been achieved. Money was short, and funds had to be raised. Parliament was not willing to give permission for the port to be built. But in the end all difficulties were overcome. Portmadoc had its harbour, and by 1812 the work was completed. Maddocks reclaimed about 10,000 acres of land from marsh and sea, though apparently he did not make the fortune he expected to make. He died in Paris in 1828 aged 54. For some time the new port was both useful and prosperous. It was an excellent harbour for ships that come for the Ffestiniog slate. Then the slate industry declined, and as a seaport Portmadoc declined with it. Perhaps as a centre for the messing-about-in-boats enthusiasts with their yachts, cruisers, sailing boats, dinghies, catamarans and all the rest it will become busy once again. The last time I was there it was quiet; it might have been one of its quiet days.

Of all unlikely people the poet Shelley came along to give Maddocks a hand. He subscribed money (though his biographers say he could not afford to) and seems to have helped out generally as a collector of funds and, so the records say, as unofficial manager. From what I have read of Shelley, he would be the last to be a very efficient manager, even unofficial, in a practical scheme of this sort.

And thereby hangs a tale.

Shelley, his wife Harriet and Harriet's sister, Eliza, came and settled into a house, Tan-yr-allt, which belonged to Maddocks. He may have been enthusiastic to start with, but he soon got tired of the office work, and probably also of soliciting contributions.

There was a storm one February night in 1813. Shelley heard noises downstairs that he thought were made by somebody who had broken in. He took his pistols (did men keep loaded pistols handy in those days?) and went down to see what was happening. There was a man in the house. Apparently *he* had loaded pistols as well for he fired at Shelley. Shelley fired back, and the man ran away. Shelley stayed up and about four in the morning was shot at again.

Next day the poet and his family left.

End of tale.

*But*—who? Why? How?

Harriet and Eliza were there and saw the bullet holes in his dressing gown so there *were* shots. It is related that Shelley really was alarmed. If that is true it was not a hoax on his part, but it would appear to be a little foolish to sit up and present himself for a target the second time.

It is a fact that he had found some neglected sheep dying on the mountain and had put them out of their misery by shooting them. By doing this he had antagonised local farmers. He was not popular;

many people believed the farmers had fired a shot or two at him to
let him know it.

But the true answer who or why has never been completely
answered.

A rather amusing sequel, related by Edmund Blunden in his
book on Shelley, is that years later a farmer owned up that he was
the one who had fired the shots. He did it to frighten the poet after
the sheep-shooting incident. The story became a tap-room joke.
But he must have been an early starter. Mr. Blunden worked it out
that he was 3 years old at the time!

The answer to this little mystery may be in an earlier letter from
Shelley (to Hogg, I believe). "I have been teased to death for the
last fortnight . . . . I allude to the embankment affair in which I
thoughtlessly engaged."

Mr. Shelley was tired of engineering.

The coastline of Caernarvonshire, the whole of the county if it
comes to that, is dominated by the Snowdon range of mountains.
People talk of Snowdon, but Snowdon is really a complex of peaks
and the height that is generally given the title is actually one called
Yr Wyddfa. Geologically I understand the formation is relatively
simple. The area which, millions of years ago, lay beneath the sea
was lifted by volcanic action into a high, wrinkled, folded-strata
plateau. Out of this, weathering and glacial action has worn out the
valleys, formed the lakes and the beds for the rivers. The harder
rocks remain and today thrust their sullen heads into the clouds, the
mists and the rains.

There in the space of a few lines is a digest of the formation of
what Pennant nearly 200 years ago labelled Snowdonia. It is somehow not the right title to my ears, but we must accept it since we do
not have a better.

Yes, a simple geological history. What it has left us with is a score
of peaks which do not vary a great deal in height as anyone can see
by looking at the range from the middle of Anglesey or some vantage
point in Denbighshire. There are about seventy square miles of
mountainous country, an eighth of the county. This is taking the
1,500 foot contour as the minimum. Half the rest is over 500 feet.
Peak lies next to peak. I know that many are rounded summits
rather than peaks, but the term will serve. Only a devoted few know
the whole system thoroughly and can distinguish one from another—
which is Foel Fras and which is Drum; which is Carnedd Llewelyn

and which is Carnedd Dafydd—or can divide Y Drosgl from Yr Aryg. And what is called Snowdon, as pointed out, is a group not a single height.

So the visitor who likes to know exactly where he is and what everything is can find things a bit of a nightmare. Perhaps Pennant was right after all. Give the lot one name and use that and leave the separate heights to the walker and the mountaineer.

Snowdon itself, Y Wyddfa, the one single Snowdon, was once Eryri, a Place of Eagles. Eagles there may have been long since, but they left or died out long ago. Occasionally one is still seen but any that come now are visitors. You would think Snowdon would have a wealth of legends and folklore associated with it, but, though the whole area is rich in old traditions, the harvest on the mountain itself is not a good one. A giant, Rhita Gawr, was buried there and it has associations with Vortigern and with Merlin. Somewhere in an unknown cave Arthur is sleeping until the day he is needed. For the rest? Well, Snowdon is Snowdon; it needs no stories to help you remember it. And wherever you go along the coasts of North Wales you seldom lose sight of it.

When you know a place well and have known it well for a long time, I imagine you get a certain feeling for it; you tend to animate it, to credit it with behaviour, with likes and dislikes; you breathe life into what is inanimate and impersonal. This is all imagination, of course. Nothing here but the rocks and the mists and the sparse vegetation. Yet personification does help you to interpret what is otherwise difficult or impossible to understand. Like everybody else, I like some places very much indeed and dislike others. Perhaps the physical features are partly responsible. So with Snowdon. I don't say I dislike it: I admire it and respect it. But I am a little in awe of it.

There is excellent cliff scenery in places along the south coast of Lleyn, which is the peninsula that thrusts south-west from the Portmadoc-Caernarvon line, and I find the extreme cape, Braich-y-pwll, almost barbaric in its grandeur. Again, there are cliffs between the bays on the north coast of the county. But the low land, as Caernarvon is approached, is Morva Harlech over again. And these wide sandy wastes, though built on in places or used for caravans and tents, grow more frequent and more spacious. On the Menai Strait the land on both sides is heavily wooded and shaded and charming, but beyond Bangor the land levels out, varying in width to be sure but there is again the memory of flat country that the sea has covered.

Here and there as at Penmaenmawr (which, though similar must not be confused with Penmaenrhos, further east) the hard rocks persist against the sea in lofty headlands, but by the time the road reaches Conway the hills are well back from the shore and there is another Morfa, Morfa Conway, level and sandy with dunes between it and the hard-sand, tide-washed beach itself. You can see a similar formation on the other side of the river Conway, for Llandudno grew on the low ground, though it has fine cliff formations in the Great Orme and the only slightly less precipitous Little Orme on the other side of the bay.

The arm of Caernarvonshire (it looks more like a leg) is called Lleyn. Just Lleyn. Once I used to call it *the* Lleyn, or the Lleyn Peninsula, but my friend Gwylim Roberts of Treffriw, who used to check all my Welsh spelling for me, since he knows more about Welsh than I do about English, said it was a title and must be used alone. So I do as I was bid.

Lleyn is a lovely part of Wales. Round the coast, as everywhere else where there are good roads these days, the holiday maker comes to the little towns, the villages, the sandy bays. Just inland the rush dies away, the noise of motors fades, and suddenly you are in country lanes, in quiet villages without so much as a souvenir or a picture postcard. From vantage points you look south over Cardigan Bay, on a clear day as far south as the Pembrokeshire cliffs and the Precelly hills. North over Caernarvon Bay you can see the low Anglesey beaches or the promentories of Holy Island beyond Holyhead. It is only a step across, say, from Pwllheli to Nevin (now Nefyn, I believe)—about the distance you would expect the energetic Arthur to fling a rock, and there are many places where you can see from Anglesey to Pembrokeshire with the Snowdon Range at your back and the Irish Sea sparkling in front. The countryside changes as the years go by, the seaside especially so as more and more visitors move in, but in places like Lleyn it proceeds only slowly and soberly. The villages, in spite of a few council houses and some new bungalows, are really much what they were. There are ancient churches, often with the characteristic North Wales double nave; the holy wells of the Celtic saints can still be found—and tried if you are dissatisfied with the National Health Service—and on the hills are cromlechs and standing stones and hill-top encampments that have not known inhabitants for 2,000 years and more. Almost anything can be found in Lleyn.

Both Tremadoc and Portmadoc owe their names to the Maddocks who reclaimed so much of the Glaslyn estuary. Pennant, who was practically on his own ground here, does not mention either place, so, unless they were very small hamlets, they hardly existed when he rode by. At the same time there is a curious tradition that links the district with a much earlier Madoc, so the embankment builder may not be the sole reason for the names.

In the twelfth century the King of Powys was Owain Gwynedd. He had four sons, and when he died the kingdom, as laid down by the law of gavelkind (division of an inheritance) was shared among them. Madoc ap Owain Gwynedd was the youngest and to him came the bare mountainous region round Snowdon.

Madoc was not happy with his portion, and he decided to do something for himself. The bards had sung a legend at least as old as the Norsemen that over the ocean to the west there was a great unknown country. Madoc thought that might well be true so he gathered together a fleet and followers and sailed into the unknown.

Long afterwards, the story goes, he returned, and so good were the accounts of the country he had discovered that hundreds, some say thousands, of his subjects joined him when he sailed away again.

Never spoil a good story for the want of a bit of decoration. Madoc and his people eventually settled in Mexico, and from the Welsh prince descended the Aztec dynasty to which Montezuma belonged.

It is a pleasant legend, but scholars have come to treat it as a joke, and no doubt in its more picturesque details it is. But if Norsemen could take their galleys across the Atlantic, and in our own time men have rowed across in much frailer craft, I see no reason why a few adventurous Welshmen should not have done the same thing.

There is a rather odd little sequel I read somewhere.

A Kentucky paper, *Paladium*, in its issue for 12th December 1805, contained a long, apparently well-authenticated account of the travels of a Welsh immigrant called Maurice Griffith. He was exploring in 1770 when he was taken prisoner by a war-party of Shawnees near Vosses' Fort at the head of the Roanoke River. They took him back to their camp and were going to put him to death. Griffith had been brought up in Wales until he was 17 years old, and he spoke Welsh. To his surprise he found he could understand the language the

Shawnees were speaking. So he began to talk to them in Welsh—and they understood him. He explained to them that he was a traveller searching for the source of the Missouri and was neither doing nor intended any harm. The Indians were so moved at their speaking the same language, or languages very similar, that they spared his life and treated him as an honoured guest.

The seashore from where the Glaslyn runs into the sea south of Portmadoc makes a curve seaward and then, in a couple of wide bays, reaches Criccieth. Not far from Portmadoc is the little watering place of Borth-y-Gest, well sheltered by the Glaslyn estuary and Harlech Point. Criccieth is known, by name at least, to many because of its associations with David Lloyd George, whose home was at Llanystumdwy a few miles away, where he is buried beneath a simple but dignified, stone-pitched memorial, in which is a stone on which he loved to sit to look at the stream below.

I do not know what place Lloyd George will have exactly in the history books. Many people could not stand him; to others he was little short of a magician. Somebody told me, "He could charm the dicky-birds out of the trees". Perhaps he is still too close to our own times for us to decide his true stature. That cannot be said of an earlier Criccieth man, Hywel y Fwyll, constable of Criccieth Castle in the fourteenth century. He fought so well at the Battle of Poitiers that the Black Prince knighted him on the field and, since his weapon had been a pole-axe, he was afterwards known as Sir Hywel of the Axe. When Hywel died the Black Prince ordered that from that time a dish of meat was to be offered before the warrior's axe every day. Now that does sound a rather useless sort of memorial, but indeed it was not. Since the axe could not eat the meat it was, after the ceremony, given to those who could, the poor. Further, "eight yeomen attendants were constituted to guard the mess, and had eight pence a day constant wages, at the King's charge".

Eight pence a day! Not bad for those times. The custom went on, Pennant said, for 200 years. Another account I found stated that the meat and the pay were still being distributed in the reign of Elizabeth I.

Pwllheli, two bays or half a dozen miles along the coast, also has associations with Poitiers. It was given to Nigel de Loring (or Lorraine) by the Black Prince for his services in the battle. Nevin, on the north coast, was also included in the gift. Pwllheli paid Nigel £14 a year, Nevin £32. In return for all this Nigel paid the Crown a heriot (token payment) of one rose a year. His name still lives in the little bay Porth Nigel, and we can only hope Nigel had a better temper than his bay, for it can be more than boisterous at times, which is why its other name is Hell's Mouth.

Pwllheli (which means Salt-water Pool) was once a port of local importance, but silting was always a problem, and though dredging was carried out it was never wholly successful, and the town is more of a seaside resort now than a seaport.

This is the last town on the way to the south-west. The villages are growing to meet the needs of the holiday makers, but at a moderate rate only. At the beginning of the century, when A. G. Bradley was writing his *Highways and Byways*, the road practically ended at Abersoch, though "the one upon which the mail cart travels the ten miles to Aberdaron, and that we must follow, is not wholly bad and is perfectly feasible for cyclists".

*Not wholly bad!* It should not have been, for through the centuries thousands of pilgrims have travelled it on their way to the Isle of the Saints, Bardsey Island.

In Lleyn you read and hear a good deal about the Pilgrims' Road, but which is the Pilgrims' Road? I have never been able to find out for certain, since it is not mapped out with the clearness of the London-Canterbury track that took people to the shrine of Thomas à Becket. Here there are two clear roads, one on the north coast and one on the south, and down the middle some byroads and country lanes, many of them hilly. If the pilgrims came by this central way they were in no hurry, for the roads go to and fro as they like.

No, I think the saints who came to die on Bardsey, or were brought to be buried on Bardsey, and the pilgrims who came to pray on Bardsey came by all the roads, those from a distance perhaps choosing the northern route, since that one, barring a little lofty unpleasantness at Permaenrhos and Penmaenmawr had a fairly uninterrupted gradient most of the way from Chester.

"Bardsey," says J. E. Lloyd, who wrote *Carnarvonshire* (1911) for the Cambridge County Geographies, "is the largest and best-known of the islands of Carnarvonshire."

Best known, indeed! A very modest understatement. It must have been the best known of the islands of Wales, of Great Britain; one of the best-known in the Christian world. This is Ynys Enlli, Benlli's Island, the Island of the Current. It has been called the

Rome of Britain, the Gate of Paradise. Three pilgrimages to Bardsey were equal to one to Rome. Merlin brought the Thirteen Treasures of Britain here, and here he sleeps, like Arthur on Snowdon, waiting for the day when he is needed. It is *Insula Sanctorum*: 20,000 saints are buried in its soil, which made Fuller say that it was easier to find graves for so many saints than saints for so many graves. Giraldus stated that "either from the wholesomeness of its climate . . . or rather from some miracle obtained from the merits of the saints, that the oldest people die first . . . and scarce any die except from extreme old age".

He may have been right too. If ever there was a peaceful spot it was Bardsey. J. E. Lloyd (quoted above) wrote,

Owing to the difficulty of the passage, communication with the mainland is uncertain and irregular, and many of the younger inhabitants have never left the island. In return it enjoys some immunities; tithes, rates and taxes are almost unknown, and it is not disturbed by the turmoil of parliamentary elections.

That was 1911. Happy days! But I understand it has not changed as much as you might expect.

The pilgrims came as far as Aberdaron, the delightful little village in Aberdaron Bay. There they rested at *Y Gegin Fawr* (the Big Kitchen), and there they took a meal, before embarking for the short but often rough and sometimes dangerous couple of miles by sea. Pennant made the journey. He did not have a great deal to say about the sacred nature of the island, but he did write that "the mariners seemed tinctured with the piety of the place: for they had not rowed far, before they made a full stop, pulled off their hats, and offered up a short prayer."

Countless thousands of pilgrims must have made this short but rough sea trip through some of the nastiest currents in Welsh waters, yet strangely, I have not been able to find any record of boats being swamped or of lives lost.

There is now a road of sorts out to the cliffs and the promontory, Braich-y-Pwll. Not the whole way but most of it. From the cliffs you can look down into a dingle where, long ago, there was a little church, St. Mary's, which was built from the offerings of pilgrims. It has vanished completely, yet one spring day I stood there looking down where the grass and the young bracken had started to grow. Only where the walls of the church had been, growth was delayed and the outline of the building stood out as clearly as it must have

done when the builders dug its foundations. A few weeks later it
would not have been visible. In winter it might be, but few would
visit this lonely spot in winter when the wind would be blowing in,
cold and salt-laden, off the sea.

There is a well on the shore below, covered at high water but
filled by a spring when the tide goes out. If you go down to the well,
fill your mouth with water, come up and run three times round the
church without spilling or swallowing any, your wishes will come
true.

I didn't try. Not that I have not a wish or two. It was the energy
I lacked.

Out at sea Bardsey lay, humped and dark and the water in the
strait broke and foamed hungrily as the tides twisted their way
through. I do not think I know any spot quite like this; it is almost
frightening, the thought of so many saints and we such sinners!

There is a lovely little church in Aberdaron, double-naved, and
in storms the sea must come up to its walls

> Now the great winds shoreward blow;
> Now the salt tides seaward flow;
> Now the wild white horses play,
> Champ and chafe and toss in the spray.

In the Middle Ages, Aberdaron Church had the privilege of
sanctuary, and a fine old row there was when an order was made
that Gruffydd ap Cynan, Prince of South Wales, who had taken
refuge, should be delivered to Henry I by a North Wales prince.
There was such an outcry against this violation that Gruffydd was
allowed to remain, and in the end he made his way back to his own
place and safety again.

Eccentrics, the genuine articles, have usually been found among
the rich who could afford to do as they liked. Such men as Jack
Mytton, the Merionethshire squire, who once overturned a pony
chaise merely because his passenger had never been upset out of a
pony chaise. Another time he intentionally set the tails of his shirt
on fire. And there was a squire in Newtown who liked to keep his
dead wives in his bedroom—which must have been slightly dis-
concerting for the current one.

Well, Aberdaron's eccentric would stand comparison with the
best of them and he was as poor as a parson's donkey. He was
Richard Robert Jones, son of the village carpenter, and he was,
and still is, known as Dic Aberdaron. He was useless at his father's

The Little Fields of Lleyn at Aberdaron
The Great Orme, Llandudno

trade, or any other, but he was a genius at picking up languages. He started with Latin and Greek and then went on to learn any that he came across. It is said that he learned thirty-five.

Other men have learned many languages but none of them can compare with this village boy turned philologist. He had no axe to grind; he was not wanting to make a living from his gift; he had no interest in the literature of the tongues he learned. All he wanted was the grammar and the vocabulary. They said he would read through a book in a language he had learned and not have any idea of the contents.

He became a tramp; he dressed in rags, was decrepit, ungroomed and dirty. A lot of people tried to help him; some gave him work, many lent him books. He studied the books but ignored the work. "He was too filthy in person for the inside of a decent house," wrote one writer, "and so bizarre in appearance that he was the butt of street boys throughout his whole long life." He wore all sorts of strange cast-offs: at one time he had trousers far too large, a huntsman's pink coat and a top-hat; at another period he went round in a blue and silver cavalry jacket and a cap of hare's skin with the ears sticking up. There are drawings of him in some of his more odd costumes. He wandered far and near, would sometimes vanish for a while, but sooner or later would be back in Lleyn, perhaps reciting some Hebrew scriptures to an astonished audience in a village street. The only constructive work he ever did was the compilation of a dictionary in Welsh, Greek and Hebrew. It was never published, and the manuscript is now in St. Asaph's Cathedral. It was at St. Asaph's he died, and it is there, in the parish churchyard, he was buried in 1843.

The coast runs north-west from the cliffs facing Bardsey, small bays alternating with fine cliffs. But round the little cape known as Carreg du (Black Rock) is a natural harbour, Porth Dinllyn, which is a fine shelter from the south-westerly gales that come roaring up the Irish Sea. Nevin is growing in popularity as a holiday resort and there is a good beach. The road draws a little inland from the sea passing through small villages, forsaking it entirely as it passes Yr Eifl (Englished into The Rivels) that faces the ocean in tall cliffs. On the eastern peak of Yr Eifl is the most important hill top fort in North Wales. The road turns northward again at Llanaelhairn, where the church is dedicated to St. Aelhairn, a name meaning Iron Brow. The iron brow was inserted by St. Beuno, who put Aelhairn

Caernarvon Castle

I

together again after wild beasts had torn him to pieces. St. Beuno could not find the forehead so he improvised with a piece of iron. It sounds difficult, but the Celtic saints did that sort of thing. St. Beuno did something like it (putting back a severed head) for St. Winifred at Holywell. Mind you, we mock at these stories, but modern surgeons perform similar operations, I heard of one who put an arm back, but the saints did them as a matter of course and made less fuss about it.

At Clynnog fawr where there is a church full of interesting old relics—"the fayrest church of all Cairnarvonshire" said Leland— the hills begin their retreat again until, as you approach Caernarvon, the Snowdon range is seen across a wide lowland plain. How gently the great skyline curves from height to height. You'd think this to be surely the most innocuous range of mountains in the world— and how wrong you would be.

Caernarvon is a fine old town with a fine old castle. Apart from its use as a slate port, which was not very early in its history, I think the Welsh put it where it is out of perverseness. The Romans built their city, Segontium, on the hill. A very good place too for those uneasy times. So the Britons, when the legions went home, settled at the foot of the hill.

Well, perhaps not. Things are seldom as simple as that. But, as I suggested in an earlier chapter, the natives seldom liked the cities and towns the Romans left behind, and in any case the Welsh have always preferred spaced-out country settlement to the confinement of towns.

Caernarvon is almost pure history. It was for centuries the head-quarters of the Welsh resistance to the Normans. Curiously, the greatest pride of what could have become a quiet little market town, its castle, was built by the enemy. Probably there had been some sort of settlement, some sort of defence here for centuries, but the first strong fortress was erected by Hugh Lupus, Earl of Chester. The present castle was one of the chain of castles planned by Edward I. "The finest ruin in the British Isles", it has been called. Even Dr. Johnson, like the ranks of Tuscany, could scarce forbear to cheer. "An edifice of stupendous majesty and strength. I did not think there had been such buildings: it surpassed my ideas."

"It looked," said H. V. Morton, seeing it in the evening, "as though a great flourish of trumpets had just died over it."

The best story of the castle is the one about the first Prince of Wales.

Edward I, wearying of the ceaseless struggle against the Welsh, in which he won the battles and the Welsh gave him hell in the guerilla struggles between, met the Welsh princes at Caernarvon to try to work out a compromise.

"Will you," he asked them, "accept as an overlord prince, one who was born in Wales, has never lived outside Wales, and cannot speak a word of English."

That seemed a fair proposition and they agreed.

Then Edward sent for a waiting nurse, and she came in carrying the son born that day to his wife, Queen Eleanor.

"Here he is," said Edward and the Princes, though they had been tricked, agreed to keep their word.

I have summarised the story. It is good for a chapter in any school history book and many times have I read it, and many pictures have I looked at pleasurably, with noble, armoured Edward, the infant prince—often carried on a shield, the kneeling Welsh chieftains swearing homage to their overlord. It is a good story with a beginning, a middle and a strong, dramatic end.

Some people say it never happened like that. One historian described sullen angry crowds in Caernarvon streets when the first Prince of Wales was proclaimed. I don't think that is much nearer the truth. I feel the story is true in that it does typify a longing for peace and an end to the to-and-fro harrying and struggling, killing and pillage. The Welsh people like most hill-people, are excellent fighters, but they are not warriors. There is a Welsh word *hiraeth* that has no easy English translation, but which means a longing sort of home-sickness. They would rather be on the hills and in the valleys than go winning battles. I am trying to simplify something I feel rather than know. But it comes to this, there are no great generals born to this people. You will not find either Wellingtons or Napoleons on these coasts.

> Why, Lord, didst Thou fashion
> Cwm Pennant so fair,
> And the years of a shepherd so few?

Poor Prince Edward! I think his adopted people must have been kind to him. Gilbert Stone in his *Wales* says he found happiness in his principality. That is more than he enjoyed later in his kingdom.

I was having a drink in the 'Prince of Wales' when who should walk in but that noble exponent of the art of *hwyl*, Tomos.

"Hail to thee, blithe spirit!" I said, or words to that effect, as I ordered him a drink.

But Tomos was not at all blithe. In fact he was distinctly moody and cast-down. It seems he had been appointed to a Caernarvon school, and, though he was teaching in English, most of the conversation was in Welsh, and they did not think much of his South Wales Welsh. In fact they made fun of it and said he *couldn't* speak Welsh, not real Welsh.

"I think I'll go back down South, mun," said Tomos. "This lot up here, their hearts are as hard as their slate."

Now I won't go deeper into this question, or *I* shall be getting rapped knuckles, but the North Wales man *does* say the South Wales man speaks only a corrupted form of Welsh, and not a very good corruption at that. And what the South Wales man says of the North Wales man *and* his Welsh will not bear repetition.

But a few beers raised Tomos's spirits quite a bit.

"And what gem of English literature have you been doling out to the babes and sucklings?" I asked.

"Oh, just the usual old things."

I'd seen the look in his eye. "Come on," I said. "Let's hear it."

"Well, indeed mun, it was real funny-like. This day I'd been telling Standard I the story of Lady Godiva."

I knew it. I *knew* it!

"Plenty of *hwyl*?" I suggested.

"I get worked up a bit, like," he admitted.

"They enjoyed it?"

"They lapped it up."

I bet they did. The lovely lady covered with her long golden hair—and *nothing* else, trust Tomos to make that clear—riding through the streets on her great white horse.

"There wasn't a blink from 'em, mun. Not a whisper. They hadn't heard it before. And I told them about that dirr-ty beast, Peeping Tom. Having a squint, like. And I says to 'em, 'What d'you think of a dirty little hound like that?' An' they said never a blind word. Never a word."

"After your eloquence they were still watching Lady Godiva."

"Aye! Well at last one little chap in the front piped up. 'If I'd been there *I'd* have peeped.'"

I could imagine Tomos's roar of rage.

"*What*! You horrible man! What d'you mean, you'd peep?"

The little fellow was very upset by Tomos's reaction.

"But Tomos," he piped, tearfully, "I haven't ever *seen* a white horse."

When I felt a little better I asked if the boys always called him Tomos.

"The little 'uns do mostly," he said. "Why not? A few of the big chaps had another name for me, but I cured *that*."

The next I heard of Tomos was that he had gone south again to the headship of a small school in Carmarthenshire.

I sent him a card to congratulate him, and in a foolish moment added, "When you need a really dramatic story for the Upper Infants try Oedipus Rex."

I should have known better. Back came a card, "It went down lovely. Do you know any more like that?"

As a footnote I may add that *I* once guided Form IA through Rex Warner's version of that horrific tale (in *Men and Gods*), and the dear little innocents loved it.

"Smashing!" they said.

As the Menai Strait is left behind, the hills are closer again, but, except in one or two places, there is always a wide and fertile tract, through which the coast road runs, and there are sands and good beaches all the way to Conway, which is built, or grew, at a fordable spot on the River Conway a mile or so up the estuary. Morfa Conway is another of those wide, sandy, dune-protected stretches that are found in so many places on the North Wales coast.

The Menai Strait has ended at Aber. Here the sea is shallow across the Lavan Sands, which are the site of another of the endless give-and-take struggle between sea and land. Under the water lies a palace, Llys Helig, and the level acres it stood on. Some authorities have cast doubt on this story, but dressed stone has been taken from the sea at low tides, while people claim to have seen ruins where the water is shallowest. The tradition is persistent, and behind tradition there is usually some truth, even if the truth is not exactly the tale told by the romancers.

It is certainly a fact that coaches for Anglesey went three miles across the Lavan Sands and then crossed the last part to Beaumaris by a ferry. It was a part of the journey that could hold some risk, and in Aber church there is a bell that was rung in misty weather to guide travellers across the sands.

Llewelyn the Great had a palace at Aber, and he brought William de Breos to it when he had taken him prisoner. Llewelyn's wife was Joan, the daughter of King John. She and de Breos fell in love. After the Norman had been released on ransom Llewelyn found out what had happened. He invited de Breos to a banquet and as soon as the knight arrived accused him of the seduction of his wife, then immediately had him hanged.

The bards told the story in verse. Pennant gives a translation of the dramatic end of the story. A bard asked Joan, "Tell me, wife of Llewelyn, what would you give for a sight of your William."

The Princess answered, "Wales, England and Llewelyn to boot, I would give them all to see my William."

So they showed him to her.

Conway has a good harbour, a bridge (two bridges now) and one of the finest of Edward I's castles. The town contains the oldest house in Britain and the smallest house in Britain, a lovely old church, and town walls which in places are fourteen feet thick. Pearls have been found in the river mussels, and, of all unlikely contrasts, the little port was in the eighteenth century noted for the export of potatoes, which the coastal ships carried away. In some years (the figures are in an appendix in Pennant's *Tours*) over 13,000 bushels were exported.

Telford's suspension bridge was started in 1822 and opened in 1826. It served for over a century, but Telford had not dreamed of motor traffic; it had become a nightmare rather than a dream when a new bridge was planned. Happily the authorities were wise enough to leave Telford's as a companion for the new one. Before Telford's bridge there was only the ferry, and that was always inconvenient and often unsafe. Dr. Johnson complained about it; he and his party got across but the tide was wrong for the larger boat that should have carried the coach, and, as it was a race day, they could not get lodgings or even a room, and the prospect of Penmaenmawr frightened them. Pennant was another who did not like the Conway ferry. Accidents happened at times. On Christmas Day 1806 the Irish Mail was upset, and fifteen of the seventeen passengers were drowned.

At Llandudno we see again the submerging of land and the emerging of it in other places. There are submerged forests to the east, yet when Tudno built his little church on the Great Orme, "on the bleakest of situations, above the sea, and remote from all dwellings", the promontory was an island. Then, presumably, an isthmus silted up. In the mid-nineteenth century there were two inns and a few small cottages. When Pennant came, roughly fifty years earlier, he did not mention even those but called Llandudno, or Orm's Head, "a beautiful sheepwalk, consisting of a fine turf, except where the rock appears, extending near four miles in length and one in breadth". On the cliffs were gulls, razorbills, "corvorants" (his spelling) herons, puffins, guillemots and peregrine falcons. "This kind was in the days of falconry so esteemed, that the great minister Burleigh sent a letter of thanks to an ancestor of Sir Roger Mostyn, for a present of a cast of Hawks from this place."

I don't think he would see many peregrines today, soaring over the sweep of bay from the Great Orme to the Little Orme. In the season, on a fine day, I don't think he would see anything—except people. Llandudno must be one of the most popular resorts in the British Isles. Not without reason, for it is, indeed, a pleasant place.

# CHAPTER 8

# ANGLESEY

THE island county was called Mona by the Romans and Mon by the natives and *Mon Mam Cymru* by the rest of Wales. That means Mon, Mother of Wales, though it is by no means agreed whether they meant they could depend on the island for a supply of food when times were bad, or, being to some degree cut off, it was regarded as a repository where their language and their culture could be kept alive. For the county *is* very Welsh in ways and tastes and language, though it also has a very individual difference from the rest of the country. But differences are the rule in islands; islanders seldom are quite like their mainland cousins.

Anglesey may have been affected by constant invasion to some extent; it is doubtful if even industrial Glamorgan has had so many visitors from so many places. Not counting the mixture that moved in before the first century, to start with there were the Romans. Few if any of those stayed, but they did have settlements, and they mined—especially for copper, and perhaps silver—in Parys Mountain in the north for hundreds of years, so it would be odd if there were not a few Italian-Celtic alliances in all that time. Irishmen came whenever they wanted adventure or spoils or refuge. Saxons came. There were constant invasions from the Scandinavian countries; those even left some names like the *ey* in Anglesey, and *holm* in Priestholm, which is another name for Puffin Island. The mixture we call Vikings were primarily invaders, but they were also land-hungry people, and some must have settled in the island. So I do not think Anglesey can say it is purely Welsh, rather that the amalgam that developed between Roman times and the Normans *became* Welsh.

And very much so. A few years ago I was at Penmynydd, the mansion-farmhouse from which the Tudors came, and I noticed three stones let into an exterior wall with some strange shapes on them.

"Is that a coat of arms?" I asked.

"No." Then joyously, "Englishmen's heads!"

Not maliciously, mind, but not without glee. A sort of "Watch your step!"

As a matter of fact it was a coat of arms, and you can find it here and there all over the island. They *were* Englishmen's heads that were cut off by a Vaughan in a battle. But the house where he had lived was a little distance from Penmynedd.

The island has the reputation of being flat, but it is not nearly as flat as it is made out to be. The land is ribbed from south-west to north-east with ridges of hard rock that give a formation of low hills and, on the coast, cliffs with sandy bays between. The most southerly trough is lower than the others, or has sunk, the sea has come in, and there you have the Menai Strait.

To the people of olden-time Anglesey this was a moat. But a moat can be crossed by determined enemies, as they discovered when a Roman army waded, swam and rowed across, defeated the natives and then massacred the Druids and cut down their sacred groves. Tacitus has told the story, but actually we know very little about the Druids in solid provable fact. We know even less about the rites they practised, except that the druids seem to have been religious leaders, and the rites were unpleasant. Religion and religious leaders must have had a strong hold on the people even so early. The Romans recognised that as long as any of the Druids were left to incite the people there would be constant unrest. Hence the massacre, and it must have been thorough, for both the Druids and their religion vanished for ever.

Pennant visited Anglesey in one of his tours (1773), though he had been there before. He crossed to the island from Caernarvon, and he mentions the Swellies, a notorious meeting point of currents as the tide flows and ebbs from both sides of the strait. "I (when very young) ventured myself in a small boat during its greatest rage, and never shall forget the rapid evolutions, between rock and rock, amidst the boiling waters, and mill-race current." To venture out on this notorious piece of water in a small boat was asking for trouble, but "when very young" we often do invite trouble, though with luck trouble does not always accept the invitation. In those times there were five ferries, originally Crown property but by then in private hands, and very profitable they were, though I believe that the 12,000 to 15,000 head of cattle (an exaggerated number, probably) he says were exported each year had to swim across. He also mentions the "incomparable" wheat he had seen growing and says that farming had improved since smuggling from the Isle of Man had been suppressed. Robbed of that profitable pastime, the people had nothing left to do but get on with their farming!

As to the strait, apart from the Swellies, he said the water was still (peaceful) at high tide, and "the rest of this strait is secure". An exaggeration, that statement, I would say. From what I know the strait should be treated with respect. There are tides coming in at each end at various times, and there are places where the water looks turbulent. I have looked at it at many places on different occasions, and sometimes there seemed to be a fine old race running. Where it is wide as it is between Beaumaris and the mainland it is grand for sailing, but I do not think I would like to swim across even if I had the strength. South of Caernarvon there are lagoons on each side, then at Aber-Menai Point the way out to Caernarvon Bay and the open sea. Menai Bridge is a small market town with a famous annual horse fair that is much older than the Bridge. It was held when the place was called Porthaethwy, and the mainland farmers, unless they were willing to pay for ferry transport (which is doubtful) had to swim their horses over whether they were buying or selling.

The Menai Suspension Bridge is surely the best known in Wales, and not altogether unknown outside it. It must have been photographed from every possible angle and is a familiar illustration in every guide book, as well as going all over the world on innumerable post cards. I expect the ferry owners grumbled more than a little when it was built, but they could hardly have had much sympathy or company.

Telford, the genius who designed it, was the son of an Eskdale shepherd. He was born in 1757 and died in 1834. He started as an apprentice to a stonemason, went to Edinburgh, then to London and finally became Surveyor of Public Works in Shropshire. He engineered the Ellesmere Canal, the Caledonian Canal, the London-Holyhead Road, St. Katherine's Docks in London, Conway Bridge and, of course, this one. It was, until recently, the longest suspension bridge in the country.

The other bridge, not far away, which carried the railway across the strait, is the Britannia Tubular Bridge, and it was built by Robert Stephenson between 1846 and 1850. This is a more solid affair and lacks the grace of Telford's structure, yet it is not unsightly, and it has served very well the purpose for which it was made.

We think of the eighteenth and nineteenth centuries as a time when rank counted for everything and the poor man kept his place.

God bless the squire and his relations,
And keep us in our proper stations.

Yet the three greatest engineers those times produced, perhaps the greatest engineers the country has ever known—James Watt, Thomas Telford and Robert Stevenson—were men of humble birth and, to start with, little education.

At the moment of writing word gets round that the Menai Bridge is not adequate for twentieth-century traffic. Let us hope that when the time comes for expansion that the old bridge, as at Conway, will get help rather than complete replacement.

A few miles from Menai Bridge is another famous name, and I include it because somebody will be cross if it is left out, though for most Welshmen the joke is wearing rather thin. The name of the village is Llanfairpwllgwyngyllgogerychwyrndrobwll-llantysiliogo-gogoch. It means "The church of St. Mary in a hollow of white hazel near a rapid whirlpool and to Tysilio's church near to a red cave".

The name is a fairly modern label, probably made up in fun, though it is an accurate description; local people are quite satisfied with Llanfair P.G.

St. Tysilio's church is a little building on land almost under the bridge, and there has been a church there since about the sixth century. It is said to be the place where Christianity was first preached in Anglesey. In those days the site was an island.

The road from Menai Bridge to Holyhead is good, straight and level. Perhaps that is how the belief arose that Anglesey is flat. Compared with, say, Snowdonia it is certainly not mountainous, but there are plenty of hills and there are valleys between. On some of the hills are the remains of the windmills which presumably ground the enormous crops of corn Pennant mentioned.

The coast is made up of what are called rock-bound bays. That is they are wide and sandy, and the rising land that surrounds them is seldom precipitous, though often higher than anyone would want to fall. On places there are some fine high cliffs. Holyhead Mountain on Holy Island rises to only 700 feet but it looks a lot more, and the Stacks, North and South, off the north-west points, show as fine cliff scenery as you will see anywhere. The north coast again has picturesque cliffs between the bays. Down the east side the land is lower, though seldom is it flat.

Still, I think you could on the whole regard the Anglesey coast as one of bays rather than of cliffs. The holiday-maker has discovered them, and the tourist industry seems to be flourishing. This must be a good thing for the island. I hope so. When I came first there was almost a depression, and a prominent citizen of Caernarvon with whom I talked said, "I don't know *what* is going to happen to Anglesey". But things have changed a lot in the last half century. A visitor in 1902 wrote, "There is not a soul here who can understand the English tongue. One might talk Hindustani with equal chance of being understood. Welsh is the only language spoken, for the bilingual Welshman is left behind when crossing the Menai."

Because nobody could give directions in English, Anglesey got a reputation as a place where tourists often got lost. Still, once they got out of the habit of cutting off Saxon heads, it was a very pleasant place in which to be lost.

Actually it was not as bad as that. It was not true that the people in the island could speak no English. Often they spoke it so badly that they were ashamed to use the little they knew, and those who could speak it well were not accustomed to think in it. I remember, years ago, asking a farm boy the way to Cefn Isaf cromlech (in Caernarvonshire). He answered me in English as good as my own (it might have been better!) but very slowly, and I was sure he was in his mind translating my question into Welsh, then translating the Welsh back into English for my benefit.

A more amusing example of a young person getting mixed up was when a purely Welsh family came to live in our village. The boy, Ivor, came into the shop one day with a pound note in his hand.

"My mother is asking if you can please to change this one-pound note for her." Pause. "She will not be minding if you do give her two ten-pound notes for it."

Well, fair enough! Who would?

Anglesey is full of ancient monuments—cromlechs, prehistoric encampments and so on. Incidentally these survivals have been catalogued and mapped and described, and I believe each county has its own volume. Some are not easy to get hold of (unless they have been reprinted since I studied them last), but they are always in the county libraries for reference.

From the shore of the Menai Strait it is worth running inland a couple of miles to Llanddaniel to see Bryn Celli Ddu which is one of the finest examples of a prehistoric burial chamber in the British Isles. It consists of a large circular mound, almost a little hill, in which, in the centre, is the burial chamber. When it was excavated, bones, both burned and unburned, were found, but they have been removed, and the passages and chamber are clear for anyone to walk through, though as it is rather out of the way not many people find it. Perhaps it is just as well. It can, except to the archaeologist, be only a relic to stare at curiously. How strange to let the mind wander back through thousands of years and realise that this was a sacred spot, that people stood here in tears, mourning and sorrowful. "Rachel weeping for her children and would not be comforted."

Not far away is a cromlech, one of the largest in the country, with a capstone twelve feet long by eleven feet wide. It may have once been covered with an earth mound as Bryn Celli Ddu still is. Why the covering should remain over one and have worn away from the other it is not easy to understand.

When Edward I was fighting his Welsh wars he decided on Beaumaris as his headquarters in this part and determined he would have a completely English town. So he moved the Welsh to the other end of the strait and called the place where he settled them, Newborough. There must have been a lot of heart-burning at the time, a lot of homesickness and unhappiness, but when you consider he could just as well have turned the natives out without making any arrangements for them, his action does not appear so heartless. Conquerors were not usually tender towards the feelings of the conquered. He gave the new Welsh town a charter so must have been doing his best not to appear too obnoxious.

Between the little town of Newborough and the sea was another wide Morfa, only this time for some reason it took the title of Warren. Sea-reeds grew widely on it, and at one time—in Pennant's day anyhow—the people of Newborough did a very good trade in ropes and mats made of these reeds. The Warren is bounded in the north by the sandy estuary known as Maltraeth Sands, with Trefdraith just north of it.

The little village was the centre of a celebrated law-suit in the late eighteenth century. The Bishop of Bangor, following the general custom of appointing English clergymen to the best Welsh livings, appointed seventy-two-year-old Dr. Bowles to Trefdraith. The

Doctor, who had a congregation of about 250, did not know a word
of Welsh. He tried preaching in English, but few of his flock were
familiar with that. There was a law, not much enforced, that divine
service in Wales should be "in the vernacular language of Wales,
with fluent and easy delivery, and a graceful propriety of accent and
prounnunciation". The doctor had a Welsh prayer book and a Welsh
Bible, so he did the best he could with those. Naturally the Welsh
"accent and pronunciation" fell short of perfection—to put it *very*
mildly! Those of his congregation who were not laughing were so
shocked that they walked out.

An action was started to get rid of Bowles, and the case came
before the Court of Arches. The parson appeared with a certificate
that his Welsh was perfect. It had been signed, as the law required,
by two churchwardens and one other parishioner. One of the churchwardens was his son-in-law; the other was a shoemaker who had
made the parson a pair of shoes and thought he was signing a receipt.
The third, Richard Williams, was not asked to read what he was
signing, but accepted the fact that the other two had signed, as
evidence that he might as well do the same.

The case lasted three years, and Doctor Bowles won it. He was
75 then and he lived a long time after, so though the people of
Trefdraith could hardly say they were sheep without a shepherd,
they could claim they did not know the shepherd's voice.

The Princes of Aberffraw must have turned in their graves. At
Aberffraw on a small inlet a couple of miles away they had a palace
to which they came for rest from their work and their wars. It has
all gone now; I do not think a trace of it remains.

Rhosneigr is a few miles up the coast and is fast growing as a
holiday resort. Then come Holy Island and Holyhead at its tip. It
grew, this town, from Caer Gybi. Why it was Caer Gybi rather than
Llangybi is a bit of a mystery, but perhaps it was a *caer* (fort) before
it became a *llan*, and it might need to be for the wild Irish loved a
frolic and a bit of pillage anywhere on these coasts.

St. Cybi was always sunburned. His friend, St. Seiriol, who
lived on the other side of the island was always pale. And this was
how it came about. The two loved to meet and talk, and on certain
days both would walk halfway across the island and meet at Llan-
erchymedd. In the morning when they set out the sun would shine
on Cybi's face, while St. Seiriol had it on his back. In the evening
when they went home again St. Cybi still had the sun on his face,

and Seiriol still had it on his back. Thus they became known as Cybi the Tawny and Seiriol the Fair.

Now isn't that a lovely story?

For centuries Caer Gybi stood there on the tip of the island, and the tumult of life passed it by and the noises it heard were the voices of the wind and the waves and the cries of the seabirds.

But it was a good place from which to depart for Ireland, so in time the roads came; and the horsemen came and the warriors and their armies, who wanted to put the wild Irish in some sort of order; and then the coaches came and then the trains came. So the town forgot St. Cybi and became noisy and full of bustle. And, though it was a mighty busy place and an important place too, this multitude of strangers passing through and then lots of coaches and then the smoky trains did its reputation no good, for you don't get any permanent good out of a lot of strangers who no sooner arrive than they are wanting to depart. All they could think of was getting through to get on with their business in Ireland, or else they were landing from Ireland with the feeling they had been in the belly of Jonah's big fish. So one way and another a lot of nasty things were said about this place.

Borrow, who could be rude enough when the occasion demanded rudeness, or even, if he felt so inclined, when it did not, was fairly civil, perhaps because the boots was a poet and admired the bards. Borrow himself admired the bards *and* would believe anybody was a poet if they told him so.

But Wesley, who was storm-bound for a couple of weeks in 1748, was bored and his preaching could do little good because hardly anyone could understand English.

Swift was downright uncivil.

Lo, here I sit at holy head
With muddy ale and mouldy bread,
I'm fastened both by mind and tide,
I see the ships at anchor ride.
All Christian vittals stink of fish,
I'm where my enemyes would wish.
Convict of lies is ev'ry sign,
The captain swears the sea's too rough—
(He has not passengers enough)
And thus the Dean is forc'd to stay,
Till others come to help the pay.

He should have gone out on to Holyhead Mountain instead of

sitting over muddy ale and writing bad poetry. On the cliffs, with a good wind blowing, nothing would have been stale, and the cries of a multitude of seabirds might have given him fresh and better inspiration.

The road from Holyhead runs roughly parallel with the coast but winds and twists a mile or so inland. There are picturesque little bays, not always easy to reach, up to the furthest north-west point, which is Carmel Head. From there you can see the small islets known as the Skerries, which have a Welsh name meaning Isle of Seals. The Skerries were valued in olden days for their fishing grounds. In the fifteenth century they belonged to Bangor Cathedral, but the Griffithses of Penrhyn (Caernarvonshire) put on one of the islands "a *Wele*, a bed or small possession". This, they claimed, gave them the fishing rights. The Bishop of Bangor retook the islands: then one of the Griffiths sons "with dyvers men in harnes, wich ryetowsely in the seid county of Anglesey within the seid bishope's diocese, took the seid fishis from the servants of the seid bishope".

The bishop prosecuted them and he won his case. Bishops usually did.

The tiny islets off the north coast are known as West Mouse, Middle Mouse and East Mouse. West Mouse is, in Welsh, *Maen y Bugail*, the Shepherd's Stone. Perhaps he threw it there. It would be a relief to find someone besides Arthur proficient at stone-throwing.

There are pleasant holiday bays all along the north coast: Cemlyn Bay, Cemaes Bay, Bull Bay. Beyond Amlwch a lane runs out nearly to Point Lynas, and a short step in from the point is Llaneilian church. This was the first church I went into on Anglesey, and I couldn't have made a better choice, for, though as I have explained in another place, I am no expert on the finer points of church architecture, I do enjoy visiting them, and I believe I have a sense of atmosphere. I'm not sure if they should be museums, but the oldest of them do seem to contain a concentration of ancient history and culture, and when they were built they often served as meeting places as well as places to worship. Often they are the only places in a parish where old things can be stored. Anyhow, if the atmosphere is right I don't think you come to much harm, and you might gain. Goldsmith had a word for it: "Fools who came to scoff, remained to pray." Not that I was scoffing.

Llaneilian church, much altered and restored, dates from the

Menai Bridge

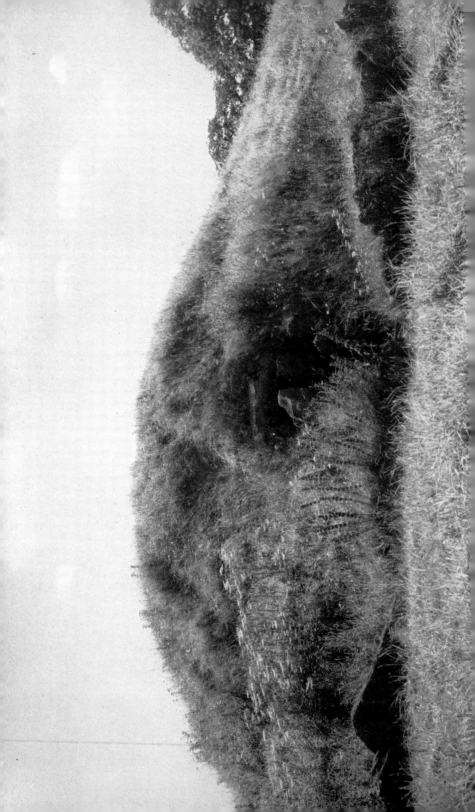

twelfth century, but St. Eilian's *llan* was here many centuries before
that. There is a fifteenth-century rood screen and a primitive painting
of a skeleton. There is an ancient portrait (presumed) of the saint.
The seats and desks are sixteenth century; the communion table
was made in 1634.

They have the old dog tongs, used not so much because they
objected to dogs in church but to throw out those who fought or
misbehaved in the usual doggy way. The iron-bound chest, *Cyff
Eilian*, was used to hold offerings from pilgrims who visited the
saint's shrine.

In St. Eilian's Chapel, separate from the church, was a little
wooden shrine and this was a great attraction to pilgrims. It was
something like a small witness box. If you could get into it and turn
round inside three times you would be cured of all diseases. Also,
doing this, and it must have been a real gymnastic trick, especially
for the not-so-slim, added five years to one's life. I have seen a
drawing of this shrine but it seems to have disappeared.

The saint's well, Fynnon Eilian, is near the church. This was a
cursing well. If you bore anyone a grudge you wrote his or her name
on a slate, attached it to a piece of cork and threw it in. As long as
it was in the well the person named would have ill health. I have
been told that some of these slates have been taken out and are still
in existence.

It doesn't sound pleasant and you wonder what St. Eilian was
about to allow it. But there's no knowing with saints; they have their
whims; they go their own ways. A cursing well would be a very
convenient medium for a poor man to, say, make things unpleasant
for a cruel landlord.

Amlwch is a mile or two back to the west and on a main road,
which Llaneilian is not. Amlwch itself lies inland a short distance
from the sea, but it has its harbour, which was blasted out of the
solid rock in the late eighteenth century to export copper from
Parys Mountain. The mountain was one of the richest sources of
copper in the world and the world market price, for a while at any
rate, depended on this corner of Anglesey. The mines have been
worked intermittently since Roman times at least. They almost
certainly used forced labour, perhaps slave labour. They seem to
have done that wherever they mined and whatever they mined for.
At times they used convicts, but the supply of those was not constant.
Taking one thing with another, the Roman occupation cannot have

Bryn Celli Ddu (Burial Chamber) Anglesey

been a very happy time for Anglesey peasants. Perhaps not for British peasants anywhere, though I think the Romans did, provided everybody behaved themselves, allow the people they conquered to mind their own business. Even when the mine owners themselves were natives I do not think they were always exactly open-handed with their workers. A rector of Amlwch, the Reverend Lemuel Jones, told me years ago that when the mines were at their most prosperous, some time in the eighteenth century, a miner's wage was only fourpence a day. It was the Rector who showed me a churchwarden's copper ládle, to look at, something like a huge soup ladle. Many North Wales churches used them for taking the collection in church, though not, we will hope from people earning 4d a day.

Over the last year or two there has been talk of re-opening the Parys mines. I believe that, at the time I am writing, surveys and investigations are being made by an American company. Well, mine-working can bring prosperity; work, well-paid work is always welcome, and they cannot make the hillsides more hideous than they were when I saw them last. Amlwch is a pleasant little town, full of character, and seen from far enough away Parys Mountain is another mountain. But when I went up it last, or partly up it, perhaps it was a dull day, or a cold day, or a wet day, but my memory is of loneliness, barren slopes, rocks strewn around, desertion, scarred hillsides and old desolate workings. This was the entrance to Pluto's Underworld, and far down in one of those sombre caves it did not take a very vivid imagination to hear the barking and howling of Cerberus.

From which you will gather I do not care much for derelict copper mines.

And you will be right.

There is a lane, but a very nice lane, going south from Llaneilian to join the main road at Penysarn, but it keeps well in from the coast, to join it, almost, at Dulas Bay. Now from here you can go down to Red Wharf Bay, which is a pleasant sandy beach with everything a good seaside should have: sands, boating, swimming, camping, caravan site—the lot. But before you reach the bay there is another little lane that runs down to the coast village of Moelfre. A lot more people have heard, even now, so long after it all happened, of Moelfre, than of Red Wharf Bay.

In the early morning of 26th October 1859, a Moelfre man

climbed up on his cottage roof. There had been a terrible storm in the night, part of his roof had been ripped off by the wind, and he was out at dawn to see what he could do about it. He saw—what *did* he see?

That's the queer thing. Nobody ever said exactly what he did see—a sinking ship? wreckage? bodies washed ashore? Whatever it was he was the first to know of the wreck of the *Royal Charter*, and it was he who gave the alarm.

The ship was homeward bound from Australia with a large number of passengers and a valuable cargo of gold. She was bound for Liverpool. The journey was as good as over; she was a fine ship, a steel-built clipper that should have been equal to any storm.

In the middle of that night she was wrecked. She broke into three, and ship and cargo and nearly all on board went down. Four hundred and sixty-five people were drowned.

A few, a very few people got ashore alive, but there was nobody who could say exactly what had happened or why it happened. I have never heard any explanation and I do not think there ever was a satisfactory one. The whole country was shocked by the disaster, and for a little while reporters, and no doubt a few of the ever-present sensation-seekers, came to this little corner of Wales. Among the correspondents was a young author by the name of Charles Dickens. He came about Christmas time, lodged at Amlwch, and came to Moelfre each day to make investigations. They were still finding bodies and burying them. He has left us his account in one of his less popular books, *The Uncommercial Traveller*.

The 465 people who lost their lives were buried, most of them, in the local churchyards. They were buried in such numbers that the local people, kind and sympathetic and sorrowing though they were, began to fear that there would be no place left for them when their time came.

A man on whom the burden of sorrow fell heavily was the Rev. Stephen Hughes, Rector of Llanallgo. In his churchyard many, perhaps most, of the victims were buried, and when Dickens was there he had written 1,075 letters to relatives and friends of the drowned people.

Of the cargo of gold, I have been told that some £300,000 was recovered. That left about £50,000. In recent years attempts have been made to find that but I do not know with what success.

In Llanallgo churchyard there is an obelisk in memory of those who lost their lives, and a plaque on it gives a brief account of what happened.

Dickens was not the only English author to come to this part of Anglesey. George Borrow had been only a short time before. It is not easy to date Borrow's wanderings, but *Wild Wales* was published in 1862, and I think the manuscript had then been three years with the publisher, who had not cared very much for it. He was wrong in his judgement. *Wild Wales* is over a century old now and, in spite of its faults, grows more popular all the time.

But Borrow was not in Anglesey to report on shipwrecks. " 'I go to buy neither hogs nor cattle,' said I, 'though I am somewhat of a judge of both; I go on a more important errand, namely to see the birthplace of the great Goronwy Owen'."

I think it is agreed that Borrow among his many gifts—and he had many—was not a good literary critic. As to poetry, he accepted many a rhymster's claim to be a poet as evidence that he was one; and if a man could say he was a bard as well Borrow fell on his neck, metaphorically at any rate.

Even a Welshman, Bryan Rhys, in one edition of the Welsh travels, writes: "Though no one can doubt Borrow's enthusiasm, it must be admitted that he overdoes his case for Welsh poetry."

But in his judgement on Goronwy Owen he was not so wide of the mark for once. Goronwy *was* a poet.

Poor Goronwy!

Born in 1723, he was one of three children of a very poor family who lived in the parish of Llanfair Mathafarn Eithaf, a name that itself rolls off the tongue like a line of poetry. Through the help of Lewis Morris, a well-known Anglesey man who had risen in the world, he was educated at Bangor and Jesus College, Oxford. Two things he wanted from life: a Welsh curacy and to write poetry. The poetry he did write, though it was not published in his lifetime. The curacy, except for three weeks in his own parish, eluded him. He did get one at Oswestry, then moved from one ill-paid post to another with a little schoolmastering as a side-line.

Whether his poverty made him turn to drink for comfort, or whether intemperance made him unreliable and useless as a parson, it is difficult to decide, and all accounts of him I have read try to evade the question tactfully, but the plain fact is that he drank too much.

Lewis Morris compared him with Milton, which seems a rather

exaggerated claim and no particular help to him into the bargain. Too many of these comparisons fly around. Better be a first-class Goronwy Owen than a third-rate Milton. Borrow said that after Dafydd ap Gwylim he was the greatest poet Wales had produced. He carried away from a tree near the birthplace some sycamore leaves as a memento.

"Prosperity to Llanfair," he writes as he ends his visit, "and may many a pilgrimage be made to it of the same character as my own." Amen to that! But somehow I doubt if they were or will be.

Goronwy Owen at last went to America, where Morris had found him a post as schoolmaster at Williamsburg, Virginia, at a salary of £200 a year.

His wife and baby son died on the journey out, but he married again twice. There are few details of his life in America; it was his most settled period so far as we know. He wrote little more, if any, poetry. He died in 1769 and left a cow and yearling, a gray horse, four negro slaves and two sermons. Total value, £300; value of the sermons, two shillings and six pence.

Out of Ireland travellers came from time to time. Sometimes a saint arrived to preach, but Wales had saints of its own, and usually it was the less worthy characters: raiders, pirates, men on the run because they had made things too hot for themselves on the other side of the water.

And witches. The Llanddona witches in particular.

It seems the Irish themselves had a habit when they were plagued by wrongdoers whom they did not want to put to death, of getting rid of them, as is still the habit in civilised nations, by deporting them. Their method was slightly more primitive than the one in use today. They just put their undesirables in an open boat, waited for a good offshore wind, then pushed them out to sea.

At Llanddona a boat-load of visitors landed one fine day from a boat which had no sails or oars or rudder. They could not speak Welsh, and the Welsh certainly could not speak their language. The Llanddona people were rather awed by these people, who could well have been Irish tinkers, full of the joys of spring at having escaped drowning. Seeing the Anglesey peasants did not know what to make of them they took advantage of the situation—and their hosts.

They stayed and were cute enough to keep apart from the local people. Their descendants, known as the Llanddona Witches, were for long respected and feared. The men were reputed to be smugglers. They may have been of use to contraband runners from the Isle of Man, that being a convenient intermediate stage for the running of French brandy and lace, though it is doubtful if they would have had the capital to do much themselves on a large scale. Anyhow you could never catch a Llanddona smuggler for he carried a little black fly tied up in a handkerchief, and he would turn it loose if he was in danger of being caught, and it would fly in the pursuer's eye and blind him. As for their women, they begged, and when they were refused charity they called down their famous curse:

May he wander for ages
And find at every step a stile,
And at every stile find a fall,
And at every fall a broken bone;
Not the largest; not the least bone
But the chief neck bone every time.

Needless to say, there were not many cottages the Llanddona Witches left empty-handed.

After Red Wharf Bay the coast runs out eastwards. Near Llanddona is another reminder of the great British monarch. Bwrdd Arthur was very likely a hill-top fort. Off the eastern point is Puffin Island or (less used) Priestholm. This has for centuries been noted as a breeding place of those quaint little parrot-like birds, the puffins. Pennant calls them puffin auks, but whether the ones he saw really had any relationship to the extinct auks I do not know. In my edition of the *Tours* (1810, three volumes) there is a delightful engraving of this puffin auk, and it looks to me exactly like the puffins that nested in the rabbit burrows on Telpin cliffs in south Carmarthenshire when I was a boy.

The island got the name of Priestholm because of the holy men who lived on it. It sounds as if there were some when Giraldus came by.

There is a small island, almost adjoining Anglesey, which is inhabited by hermits, living by manual labour, and serving God. It is remarkable that when, by the influence of human passions, any discord arises among them, all their provisions are devoured and infected by a species of small mice, with which the island abounds, but when the discord ceases, they are no longer molested.

I would like to believe all the stories related by Giraldus, but to be credulous it is necessary to be charitable.

"We saw in Anglesey a dog, who accidentally had lost his tail, and whose whole progeny bore the same defect." My own charity won't stretch as far as that!

The ruins of Penmon Priory are quite near the sea and the cape facing Puffin Island. The best preserved part is the dovecot. A few miles further is Llanfaes, where there was a religious house which, it is believed was founded by Prince Llewelyn in memory of his wife, Joan. Their early history, marred by her betrayal and the hanging of her lover, William de Breos, was tragic, but Llewelyn forgave her infidelity, and, according to Gilbert Stone in his *Wales*, eventually they were happy together. This historian pointed out that their marriage had been one of convenience, a political move, and he says that she had statesmanlike gifts and worked hard for unity and peace between the two countries. It is thought that Joan was buried at Llanfaes, but all trace of her grave was lost, probably after the Reformation. Then, in the nineteenth century someone had a close look at a stone watering trough in a local farmyard, and it turned out to be her coffin. Later the lid was discovered in a ditch. Coffin and lid are now in the porch of Beaumaris church. This porch also holds the original heavy drawbar that could turn the place of worship into a fortress.

Beaumaris could hardly fail to be pleasant, situated as it is, looking out over the widest and most picturesque part of the Menai Strait. From the shell of the great castle are wonderful views of the Snowdon Range. But in stormy weather and under grey skies the wind can be boisterous here, and all is not invariably sunshine and light. On the sandbanks and reefs to the east more than one ship has gone down. The most notable wreck was that of the *Rothesay Castle* on Dutchman's Bank in 1831, when a hundred lives were lost. Harriet Martineau tells a story of how two men from this wreck clung to the same piece of wood that was not big enough for both. One wanted to let go because he was old, the other because he was young. They both let go at the same moment. And both managed to get to shore and came face to face again. "Few greetings in the course of life can be so sweet and moving as must have been that of these two heroes."

But I do not want to leave Anglesey with only a memory of ship-wreck and disaster. Here is a story from Pennant's *Tour*.

I must not omit to mention the great patriarch of Tregain, a chapelry of this parish, who lived in the year 1580, and died at the age of 105; his name was William ap Howel ap Jerworth. He had by his first wife twenty-two children, by his second ten, by his third, four, and by his two concubines seven; in all forty-three. His eldest son was eighty-four in 1581, and his eldest daughter seventy-two; so that between his first child and last there was an interval of eighty-two years. Nor did there less than three hundred people descend from this stock in that interval, eighty of whom lived in this parish. He was small of stature, of a cheerful convivial temper; but spare in his diet, living mostly on milk. He passed his time in rural employments, and at his leisure in fishing and fowling; and preserved his memory and senses to the last.

# CHAPTER 9

# FROM THE LITTLE ORME TO RHYL

THE Denbighshire coast is only some dozen miles across the wide bay from Rhos-on-Sea to Rhyl, and it is better as a coast than as material for a book. That is to say, it is splendid for holidays but a little monotonous. There are fine sands, pleasant beaches, safe bathing, facilities for boating and sailing and fishing; holiday camps and camping and caravan sites, boarding houses and hotels. The whole length, and then on through Flintshire, has been developed as a holiday and touring area, and, to judge by the traffic and the crowds on any fine summer day, it has been developed very successfully. Being so near to the wonderful background of Snowdonia and the other mountains of North Wales must have been a great asset. Places that a century ago held no more than a few cottages and a score or so of people are now large towns with all the virtues and the faults and the problems that large modern towns gather to themselves as they grow.

Along this stretch conditions change almost as quickly as the weather. There is constant bustle and hurry. People are here today, gone tomorrow, making a sort of fluid population. Many English people, especially from the industrial north-west, like it so much that they retire here, settle here. Whether Wales can absorb them, as it always has absorbed newcomers, only time can tell. Ways of life have altered a lot in recent years. I am not sure that in the centres of population the purely Welsh ones have survived, though they may remain in the very rural districts for quite a long time. It seems that ways of living, and interests, are less varied than they used to be, and English, Scots, Irish and Welsh are all occupied in their leisure by Bingo, radio, television, football matches, pools and all the rest that make up today's bread and circuses. We are interested in the same things, and we grow more like each other.

When my family went to Pembrokeshire they had a choice of mixing and becoming Pembrokeshire folk themselves, or staying apart and being absolutely alone, splendid but miserable, in their

Saxon isolation. Of course they mixed. They were like that. Until I was quite a grown-up young man I didn't realise I was not really what the natives themselves called a 'Pembrokeshire Pig', and during my rare holidays in England my cousins called me Taffy.

We went there, we stayed. It was home and we belonged. Nowadays progress has arrived, and we dash around as if we were playing musical chairs. You may think all this does not matter, but it does. Parts of Wales grow more and more nationally conscious; other parts wonder what all the fuss is about and do not want either official forms or their entertainment in Welsh. When people do not stay, do not settle, it only accentuates the divisions that Giraldus deplored centuries ago.

The North Wales coast has, like all the Welsh coasts, altered a lot over the centuries. Abergele is now about a mile from the sea, but there is evidence that it was once a lot further away. There is a tablet in the churchyard wall which says, "In this churchyard lies a man who lived three miles to the north of it". This is supposed to be a translation of an inscription in Welsh, and Pennant saw it in Welsh. I do not know what happened to the original. But as a better proof of submerged land, he said,

> I have observed at low-water, far from the clayey banks, a long tract of hard loam, filled with the bodies of oak trees, tolerably entire, but so soft as to be cut with a knife as easily as wax.
> The wood is collected by the poorer people, and, after being brought to dry upon the beach, is carried home and used as fuel, but in burning, it emits a very bad smell.

The smell may have been similar to the smell of burning peat. Many people think that is pleasant.

He was rude about the church: "a long awkward pile with a high tower steeple".

The two memorials in Abergele churchyard were not there at the time of his visit. One is in memory of people lost in the wreck of the *Ocean Monarch*, which happened in Abergele Roads in 1848; the other remembers a disaster to the Irish mail train near Llandulas. That happened in August 1868 when it ran into some petroleum trucks. Thirty-three people died, and they were buried in one grave.

Curiously, A. G. Bradley, writing as recently as 1909, claimed that Denbighshire was "as Welsh in every respect worth mentioning as Cardigan and Merioneth". Today that is true only inland and away from the coast.

Things are not quite as they were in Bradley's days. Then, pretty well everybody in North Wales spoke Welsh, and a lot of people spoke nothing else. In contrast, the well-to-do, the squires, and such middle-class as there was, used English almost exclusively. Many of them had no Welsh at all, nor much interest in it. Bradley wrote at length about this in *Highways and Byways of North Wales* and stressed how important it was that the squires and landlords should know the language of the people so that they could understand their difficulties and their troubles, both of which they had in abundance. You only need to go back half a century from Bradley to Borrow's *Walks in Wales* (*Wild Wales*) to realise what utter poverty there was in many parts of the country.

For most of the Welsh peasantry there was only one way of escape from their miserable conditions and that was by educating themselves.

No wonder a hunger for education grew up in the country. In many parts it became an obsession. It was so in Cardiganshire, and it was nearly as much so right across North Wales. Get an education and you could become a schoolmaster or a parson. Not that that would mean riches, but at least you fed a bit better, and you were respected. And you could always climb further. Get an education and there was no limit. It was this spirit that was behind the hard start and the painful growth of the University of Wales.

A good example of the education hunger can be found in the village of Llangernyw and its cobbler's son. Henry Jones was born in a small cottage (still standing) in 1852, which takes us back earlier than Borrow's visits. He started life as apprentice to his father, but his great desire was to be educated. By tremendous efforts—and finding even the least money for fees must have been painful—he acquired a little elementary learning, studied to improve on it and went eventually to study at Glasgow, then at Oxford, then in Germany. Eventually he became Professor of Philosophy at Glasgow and later was knighted. He died in 1922, and I have heard more than one person in North Wales speak of him with deep respect. In fact it was a North Wales man who insisted a few years ago that I should go to Llangernyw, see the cottage and find out the facts about the scholar's life. I must confess I had never heard of him, but then it is a story that can be duplicated in many of the remote parts of Wales.

To balance it there were also in some places country people who

were sure that "all this education don't do nobody no good".
Actually they were correct as far as it referred to themselves, and
usually they were people with well-filled bellies.

Henry Jones had brains; it was too bad for the poor devils who
had none.

To some extent Bradley was right. The North Wales squires,
speaking generally of most of them, despised their own language.
And in North Wales, while the peasants understood English, nearly
all of them spoke Welsh. In South Wales most people, even when
Welsh was their first language, spoke English as well, and there was
better communication between squires and people and perhaps a
little more sympathy between them.

The North Wales gentry were a formidable lot, Wynnes and
Watkinses, Mostyns and Myddletons, Thelwalls and Salusburys
and Williams-Wynns. Many were rich, and some were powerful,
but their worldly ambitions usually were outside Wales, and the
money they took from their native country they spent away from it.
If they had stayed at home and spent their money at home there
could not have been the poverty there was. Borrow saw it as a
visitor. A Welshman who was a boy when Borrow came saw it from
the inside. He was Denbighshire born. His name was Hugh Evans
and while still young he went to Liverpool, became a journalist, a
printer and, in a small way, a publisher. He founded a newspaper,
Y Brython, and the Brython Press. His memories of his childhood
he gathered together in a book, Cwm Eithin. It was published in
Welsh by his own press and later translated into English under the
title The Gorse Glen. It gives a wonderful picture of the North
Wales of the first half of the nineteenth century. It is not a cheerless
story, in fact it is full of love and nostalgic affection; but do what he
will, poverty rears its ugly head while its offspring, sickness and
starvation look over its shoulder.

To take one point alone. Everybody who has read any history at
all knows of the dreadful suffering in Ireland when the potato crops
failed. I have met hardly anyone who knew that the Welsh peasantry
suffered in exactly the same way.

In South Wales heavy industries, coal and iron especially, were
starting. These tore the countryside to pieces and littered lovely
valleys with pit-head buildings and ugly houses. But where there is
industry there is work, and when men work, however poor the pay,
they and their families eat. People suffered a lot in the South Wales

valleys, but they did not, as a rule, literally starve, as they did in the North.

Hugh Evans had his own memories; he also (somewhat as Hardy did) drew on memories that stretched back to the Napoleonic wars. Passages from his book stay in the memory.

In addition to the devastation caused by war there was a succession of bad harvests; the weather was so bad that it was impossible to harvest the grain properly. So wet was the corn that the flour made from it could not be made into bread. . . .
Hundreds and thousands died from want and lack of proper nourishment. . . . Winter coming on and famine staring us in the face.

In one family the father undertook all the work of the house while the mother knitted stockings from morning till night, sleeping only five or six hours. "Once a fortnight my mother would go on horseback to Ruthin over Mynydd Hiraethog, a distance of some fifteen miles, with her bundle of stockings to sell to the stocking man. . . . And so it was that she kept us alive until the next harvest."

No holiday makers with full pockets came here to paddle and bathe and sail boats. No 'Bed and Breakfasts' to earn a few shillings, no tents, no caravans. We wail, some of us, about the holiday camps and ruined scenery and litter. After I read *The Gorse Glen* I seemed to see things in a different light. Better a bit of ruined scenery than starvation. "The people tried to keep body and soul together with the aid of cabbages and roots and potatoes and salt." Then came the potato blight. "That was a dreadful year in the history of Wales. I will give some instances to show how terribly hard-hearted some of the rich people were in those hard days."

Then he says, "Conditions were similar in Ireland. Thousands died of famine in Ireland. . . . There was nothing to be done except to gather herbs and leaves and with these contrive something to keep body and soul together."

A minister from Bala, preaching in this district had his dinner in an old woman's cottage. . . . "When he returned home at night his daughters were curious to know what the meal had consisted of. . . . 'If you must know,' he said. 'I had a turnip boiled with salt, and it was very good'."

Some of the squires may have given help where they could; some, out of touch, may not have known how very bad things were; some were hardly ever at home. But there were too many who just did not care, except about their rents, and the agents of those did not, or dared not, care either. Hugh Evans put the blame squarely where it belonged. Yet, he records,

> Despite the oppressive conduct of the landowners the people clung with a servile devotion to the old gentry. . . .
> The laws were made by the landlords and were unfair and oppressive. The poor man could not look for fair play or redress. . . .
> Four things were the curse of Cwn Eithin—landlordism, the land laws, the oppression of the landlord and the filching of the mountain common rights from the people.

Old unhappy far-off things. Almost forgotten. Yet they are part of the picture and should be remembered, if only to counterbalance the good-old-days nostalgia; *also* to get in focus the stories of unlimited smuggling all along the coast and the stories of the rich cargoes that were carried into the hills. I do not feel somehow that the Reverend Simon Llwyd of Bala washed down his turnip with a glass of French brandy.

While on the subject of the North Wales landlords, one of the most renowned of these families was the Salusburys, who had estates in this district and were closely associated with Denbigh itself. It is not a very Welsh-sounding name, and in fact it is not Welsh. Though they traced their descent from long before 1066, they came over with the Conqueror, settled in Wales quite early, and, through marriages to Welsh heiresses, were absorbed and became Welsh. One of the heiresses has become the heroine—to use the term *very* charitably—of a Denbighshire story. She was Catherine de Beraine, and she was a great-granddaughter of Henry Tudor (later Henry VII) and a Breton girl he loved when he was an exile in Brittany.

Catherine's first husband was the Sir John Salusbury of the time. He died after a few years. The widow was accompanied to the burial by his friend Sir Richard Clough, and Sir Richard, wasting no time, proposed to her on the way to the church. She accepted him.

On the way *from* the funeral another friend, Maurice Wynn of Gwydir, also proposed. Catherine said she was sorry but she had already accepted Sir Richard, but should she ever be husbandless again she would consider him then. Sir Richard did die and she did marry Maurice Wynn. And when Maurice Wynn died she rounded things off by marrying Edward Thelwall of Plas-y-Ward. All these men were rich with great estates, and from each marriage she raised a family. Her descendants became so numerous that the common joke against her was that she shared with Anglesey the title *Mam Cymru*, Mother of Wales.

Her first son by Salusbury had two thumbs on each hand and is known traditionally as Syr John y Bodiau, Sir John of the Thumbs. He was noted for his enormous strength and many tales are told of his feats, one of which was killing a lioness in the Tower of London. They say when he had nobody to fight or wrestle with he would pass the time by uprooting trees. He was buried at Whitchurch. A less formidable descendant of Catherine, through the Clough marriage, was Mrs. Thrale, the friend of Dr. Johnson.

Catherine lived at Henllan, which is a short run inland from Abergele. A woman so fortunate in love and estates would naturally arouse jealousy, and there are various scandals swirling smokily around her name. Bradley hints that she was unfaithful. Another story says she killed her husbands by pouring molten lead into their ears as they slept. We might allow that she grew tired of each but she would surely have found a simpler method of getting rid of them, and since the same stories tell of her finding Sir Richard Clough in the friendly company of the Devil, who had baked the bricks for his house, Bachygraig, we need not take these legends too seriously. The probability, to put it politely, is that she liked men; the certainty is that she liked estates and the fortunes they brought.

I doubt, also, the story that her last husband (some accounts say she had six; I can only trace four) suspecting that his time had come for the molten lead treatment, locked her in a room and starved her to death.

There are portraits of Catherine de Beraine in existence. Baring-Gould claimed to see something sinister and evil in the one he saw. I think he had taken the stories of her ruthlessness too seriously. I saw only a pretty woman.

One other short tale I heard about the North Wales squires. William Myddleton was the sailor who brought Admiral Howard the news of the approach of the Spanish fleet which Sir Richard Grenville fought later so bravely with the *Revenge*. And of this Captain Myddleton:

> It is sayed, that he, with Captain Thomas Price of Plasyollin, and one Captain Koet, were the first who smoked, or (as they called it) drank tobacco publickly in London; so that Londoners flocked from all parts to see them. Pipes were not then invented, so they used the twisted leaves, or segars.

The Denbighshire portion of coast starts just below Llandrilloyn-rhos, which is inclined to get lost as Colwyn Bay spreads itself. The old church of St. Trillo, which dates from the thirteenth century, is, like so many coastal churches, set back a little from the sea. By the look of the great sockets inside the door it could have been used as a refuge, or even as a minor fortress in case of a pirate raid. Down by the sea was St. Trillo's Well, which might have become lost in the twentieth-century building had not long ago a little chapel been built over it. I have been told it was erected in St. Trillo's time, a claim I doubt, though there may well have been a chapel of some sort over it through most of its history. This little chapel is unique in my experience. It is the smallest church, eleven feet by eight feet, I have ever been in, and like so many small things it is enchanting. But it is there for serious use and regular services are held in it.

Before Colwyn Bay existed this was an important place. In olden days there was a fish weir below the chapel. It belonged to the monks of Conway. At the Reformation, though accounts are not quite clear, it appears to have been handed over to the parish. Or did the parish just take it over? At any rate the tithe of fish caught belonged for a long time to the incumbent, who in return was obliged to read prayers at the weir three times during the fishing season.

Colwyn Bay is completely modern. I don't mean it is the worse for that, but modern it is. Like the rest of us it will grow older. Little more than a century ago it consisted of one house, now the Pwllcrochan Hotel. There *was* a Colwyn however, a village, now dignified by the name of Old Colwyn. This too stands back a little from the sea (many of the villages do), and the siting may be intentional. Living too close to the sea may not have been healthy. Apart from early raids from thieving Scandinavians, there was a period when intermittent piracy was a popular diversion of the Manxmen, and their island, with a good northerly breeze blowing, would not be too far away.

A couple of miles inland from Old Colwyn is Llanelian-yn-Rhos, where the church is dedicated to St. Elian. Although the spelling is slightly different, I take it he was the same man as St. Eilian of North Anglesey, because here, as at Llaneilian, there was a cursing well. Now Llaneilian (Anglesey) is much more remote than Llanelian (Denbigh), and though the well at the former was much patronised, the one at the latter had even greater fame, and more pilgrims and a scandal or two for good measure. We may smile as we read of

Beaumaris Castle, Anglesey
The north end of the Menai Strait

these simple people ill-wishing their enemies (not having any superstitions of our own!) but indeed it was no smiling matter. People believed in the misfortunes they desired to fall on others; they believed in the misfortunes they knew would fall on them. Since none of the poor people who came could have paid very large sums, they must have come in large numbers. A woman who looked after it at one time made £300 a year, getting what you might call double pay, since she received a fee from those who put a curse in the well and a reward from those who had been cursed to take it out again. Once the name was removed, usually written on slate, the curse was believed to be ineffective.

I have read that at the Flintshire Great Sessions in 1818 the 'priest' of the well was sent to prison for twelve months for obtaining money under false pretences. Pennant, who was as reliable a guide as we have to those times, relates how someone threatened to curse him at this well. He was not alarmed: credulous people were.

In the end a rector, tired of the superstitions and the cheating, had the well filled in.

Cursing wells were so rare that they were curiosities. But healing wells were common all over the country. Perhaps they are common all over the world; wasn't there one at Bethesda? . . . . There was some magic in water that sprang up out of the earth. Often the magic worked. The magic that was not only in the water but in the faith that brought people to it.

One of the best-known Denbighshire wells was at Llandegla near Ruthin. In olden days it was noted for curing epilepsy. It was still in use when Pennant visited it, and here is his account of the ceremonial that took place:

> The patient washes his limbs in the well; makes an offering into it of four pence; walks round it three times; and thrice repeats the Lord's prayer. These ceremonies are never begun till after sunset, in order to inspire the votaries with greater awe. If the afflicted be of the male sex, like Socrates, he makes an offering of a cock to his Esculapius, or rather to Tecla Hygeia; if of the fair sex, a hen. The fowl is carried in a basket, first round the well; after that into the churchyard; when the same orisons, and the same circumambulations are performed round the church. The votary then enters the church; gets under the communion table; lies down with the Bible under his or her head; is covered with the carpet or cloth, and rests there till the break of day; departing after offering sixpence, and leaving the fowl in the church. If the bird dies, the cure is supposed to have been effected, and the disease transferred to the devoted victim.

View from Bryn Euryn of Colwyn Bay

L

Some of this comes pretty near witchcraft, but at the majority of wells the ritual was simple. You drank or bathed or perhaps prayed; you dropped a trifling fee, often a pin, into the well. That was all. It did no harm; for many people there was the reward of a small miracle. Or so it seemed. In times of more simple faith, and when no other help was available, the number of sick people who visited the wells must have been enormous. I know of wells in Herefordshire where great lumps of pins, all rusted together in one mass, have been cleaned out.

Before the coast sinks to the level sandy shores that are characteristic all the way to Point of Air and the turn south into the Dee estuary, there are one or two places where the rocks come rearing through. After the Little Orme the best-known is Penmaenrhos between Colwyn and Llandulas. Modern road engineering has reduced its terrors to nothing, though there are some fine heights to look down from a few vantage points on the top, and the view east and west stretches from Anglesey to the Dee. But until modern times Penmaenrhos was a hazard to be feared on a journey across North Wales.

It figures in the last miserable scenes of Richard II's tragic story. His army deserted when he got to Wales, but the Welsh were largely on his side had he known exactly what to do or what he meant to do. By the time he got to Conway he was virtually without forces. Bolingbroke, remaining at Flint, sent the Earl of Northumberland to fetch him, and Northumberland left his men to wait on the east side of the headland. Why he did this is not clear unless he thought Richard might yet get together a Welsh army. Northumberland pretended friendship; Richard did the same. It is said they swore before the altar in Conway church that they meant well to each other. That, if true, makes one wonder how much the piety of those days meant. Northumberland was luring Richard into a trap; Richard intended if he could get Bolingbroke in his power to "put him to such a cruel death that it should be spoken of even in Turkey".

So they set out, and when they crossed the hill at Penmaenrhos there were the Earl's troops. Richard must have realised that other men besides he could swear false oaths.

Dr. Johnson wrote in his diary in which he was recording his journeys in Wales,

To spare the horrors at Penmaen Rhos between Conway and St. Asaph we sent the coach over the road across the mountain with Mrs. Thrale, who had been tired with a walk sometime before, and I, with Mr. Thrale and Miss, walked along the edge, where the path is very narrow and much encumbered by little loose stones, which had fallen down, as we thought, upon the way since we passed it before.

The coach road went behind the headland. Foot passengers had a track near sea level. Nobody between Johnson and Pennant had gone to the trouble of making it safer or more attractive.

"Penmaen Rhos, a great limestone rock juts into the sea at the end of the bay," wrote Pennant. "In my memory the traveller went along a narrow path cut on its front, like the road on Penmaen Mawr, but infinitely more terrible and dangerous."

Dr. Johnson made a journey into North Wales with Mr. and Mrs. Thrale about 1774. She had been born at Bodfael Hall in Bodfaen and, as mentioned earlier, was a descendant of Catherine of Beraine and the Clough family. She had inherited a small estate from some of the Clough relations and, having to come down to see about it, brought Dr. Johnson for a holiday and so that he could see how beautiful her native country was. Bradley mentions his "affable behaviour as he rolled about the parlours" (of the Denbighshire squires), which he said was "a matter of history which everyone should look up who is setting his face towards the Vale of Clwyd".

Did Bradley look it up himself, I wonder. The history is contained in Johnson's diary of his tour, a comparatively rare volume which I think was not widely circulated nor reprinted. After reading it I did not have the impression of affability. I do not think he was in the best of health at that time, and I do not think he was in the best of moods either. He was not a man who enjoyed long country walks, and scenery he seemed to find a bore. Johnson was a man who was at his best with his feet under a table, wine and food before him and his friends around.

He was taken to see a famous waterfall and was not interested. "I trudged unwillingly and was not sorry to find it dry." His notes were brief and unenthusiastic. Many places he saw and many buildings he visited he dismissed as mean. He admitted Wrexham was "a busy, extensive and well-built town", but he records the fact rather than admires the place.

He went to church and went so far as to admit he did not dislike the sound of Welsh. "At Bodfari I heard the second lesson read and the sermon preached in Welsh. The text was pronounced both in

Welsh and English. The sound of the Welsh in a continuous discourse is not unpleasant."

He stayed at Gwaenynog near Denbigh, but one of the most interesting towns in North Wales made hardly any impression on him. "How we spent our time I am not very able to tell." But he did make a note about men looking for work in the harvest fields. He saw them on Sunday: "I saw the harvest-men very decently dressed, after the afternoon service standing to be hired. On other days they stand at about four in the morning. They are hired from day to day."

Unfortunately, his host, one of the Myddletons, gave offence. Wanting to do the Doctor honour he had an urn put up in his grounds with an inscription which said, "This spot was often dignified by the presence of SAMUEL JOHNSON, LL.D." Johnson might have swallowed the flattery, but the urn spoiled all. "Mr. Myddleton's erection of an urn, looks like an intention to bury me alive; I would as willingly see my friend, however benevolent and hospitable, quietly inurned. Let him think, for the present, of some more acceptable memorial."

At Bangor, "a very mean inn . . . I lay in a room where the other bed had two men".

Only to Boswell did he praise Wales . . . "instead of black and barren mountains, there were green and fertile ones."

At least it was better than Scotland.

After Penmaenrhos the coast falls to the sandy beaches. The sea is more shallow and the hills are further from it, though always they make a beautiful background. All the way to Point of Air is a growing playground for half the north of England and some of the South of it and much of Wales. Here again the sea has taken wide stretches of the low-lying land. Exactly how much and when, it is difficult to decide, but much later, I imagine, than the loss of Cantref y Gwaelod. Speed's maps, drawn in the early seventeenth century and very accurate for his time, shows the coast from Point of Air westwards as being in some places a mile or two out where now there is sea. There is also a surmised coatline as it was thought to be in the second century, and that is still further out. On what evidence that coast is fixed I do not know. There were Roman settlements at Chester and in Flint, but I have never heard of any written record being left.

Eastwards from Abergele is the wide plain known as Morfa

Rhuddlan. Widening, triangular-shaped, it stretches for some miles up to the border of Flint and extends down to Rhyl on the coast again. A little stream, the Gele, divides it on its sluggish way to Abergele. The marsh is

> celebrated for the battle in 795 between the Saxons and the Welsh: our monarch Caradoc fell in the conflict, and, I fear, victory declared against us. We do indeed say, that Offa, the famous king of Mercia, was slain here; but the Saxon chronicle places his death the year before that battle. The fine plaintive Welsh tune, so well known by the name of *Morfa Rhuddlan*, is supposed to have been composed on this occasion: for victories are not the only subjects for the harp.

The coast of Denbighshire is not, except for the holiday-maker, very interesting, but off the coast road the countryside can compare with any part of Wales. Twenty miles or so to the south is the A5, carrying the crowds hurrying towards Snowdonia. There is a good road on the western boundary, taking people to Llandudno and the resorts near it; another on the east, bound for Rhyl. In the rectangle formed by these roads is the quiet country, the hamlets, the farms and cottages, the rivers and the hills. The mountains of Caernarvonshire fall after the River Conway to the gentler slopes of Mynydd Hiraethog and, further south and east, the Berwyns. From the sea the land rises more and more gradually, and generally to moorlands and uplands rather than to wild, inhospitable heights. Mynydd Hiraethog is well below 2,000 feet, and, with its lakes and Alwen reservoir, is the least cultivated area, being given over mainly to sheepwalks.

The towns are full of interest. Wrexham is large but rather far inland. But Ruthin and Denbigh, full, both of them, of historic interest are only a short distance from the sea. Everybody liked Ruthin—and said so: Camden, Borrow, Leigh Hunt, Landor, Bradley were among those who sang its praises, while Stanley Weyman who lived and died at Llanrhudd nearby, wrote, "Rhyl, St. Asaph, Denbigh and Ruthin lie along the Vale of Clwyd like beads threaded on a string and the fairest of these is Ruthin."

Denbigh had its castle, one of the last to hold out for King Charles, and earlier there was a Priory of White Friars. Sir John of the Thumbs was buried at St. Marcella's nearby, and so was Twm o'r Nant, who wrote the folk-plays known as *Interludes*. "He is called the Shakespeare of Wales", said an old woman who showed his portrait to Borrow. The explorer, H. M. Stanley, was born in a cottage under the Castle walls. Hugh Myddleton, who engineered London's water supply in the seventeenth century was a Denbigh man, and one of his brothers became a Lord Mayor of London.

In the country lanes there are delightful villages, and in nearly every one there is a feature to make it worth a visit; an old church, or a well, or a reminder of some famous person. Richard Wilson painted the inn sign at Loggerheads and, though he was Montgomeryshire born, he died at Loggerheads and was buried at Mold. Llanfair-Talhairn celebrates another Ironbrow. Perhaps St. Beuno worked a similar miracle here to the one he performed in Lleyn. At Llanrhaidr there is a holy well that is famous for curing skin diseases, but the great pride of the place is the beautiful stained-glass Jesse window which the parishioners took to pieces and buried in a neighbouring wood to save it from destruction in the Civil War. Jesse windows, which are rare, show Jesus as an offspring of David's father, generally on a tree springing from the old man's side.

> And there is the gravestone with the inscription: Heare lyeth the body of John, ap Robert of Porth, ap Robert of Porth, ap David, ap Griffith, ap Jerworth, ap Llewelyn, ap Jeroh, ap Heilin, ap Cowryd, ap Cadvan, ap Alawgwa, ap Cadell, the King of Powys, who departed this life the XX day of March, in the year of our Lord God 1642 and of his age XCV.

I wonder if this pedigree, and similar ones, explains the folk tale I heard. It is not a specially good folk tale, but I could not at first see how it was worked out, and another interesting feature is that I have not heard it duplicated.

You have to bear in mind that *ap* is the equivalent of *son of*, while *a* in Welsh means *and*. So John ap Howell ap Evan etc, could be John a Powell a Bevan . . . etc., which is John and Powell and Bevan . . . and so on.

A man going home one dark night heard a voice calling for help. When he went to find out who it was he discovered that somebody who had had too much Welsh home-brewed ale had fallen into a deep ditch and could not get out.

"Who is it?" he asked.

Welshmen are proud of their long pedigrees. The voice replied. "John and Powell and Bevan and Richard and Rees and Robert . . . ."

"If there's all that lot of you there, help each other out and don't bother me," said the traveller as he went on his way.

This story belongs to both Denbigh and Flint and there is a good harvest of folk lore to be gathered in both countries, but most of them are very similar to their duplicates in other places, and a few, though I do not think they could be derived from Grimm, are almost identical to similar stories in the famous *Fairy Tales*.

You do find what I call 'Ploughboy Stories', the sort of anecdotes the young farm servants would tell, sometimes with bawdy embellishments, on a winter evening, or, if they ever had them, in their idle moments.

This sort of thing:

A boy was hired as a servant on a farm. After he had been there a few weeks a cow took ill.

"Kill it," said the mean old farmer.

For some time to come everybody lived on salt beef.

Then the pig took ill.

"Kill it," said the farmer.

For weeks they lived on salt pork.

Then a ewe took ill.

"Kill it," said the farmer.

They feasted, if that is the word, on salt mutton.

One day the shepherd met the boy leaving the farm as fast as he could go, his bundle over his shoulder.

"Where be'est 'ee off to?" asked the shepherd.

"I'm leaving," said the boy. "The missus is just took sick."

Back on the coast, of course, the stories are of the fine cargoes that used to come down from the Isle of Man. Maybe they did. But I don't think the tellers of stories in candle-lit cottage kitchens got much profit from them. Folk lore is for folk; contraband is for those who can pay for the goods and for the risks.

# CHAPTER 10

# RHYL TO THE DEE

THE County of Flint has only a short coastline facing the ocean. From Rhyl to Point of Air is about eight miles as the crow flies. Then there is another length, some sixteen miles or a little more, along the Dee estuary, turning to the east of it for a short distance beyond Connah's Quay. The coast proper is very much the same as it is in Denbighshire: sea and sands, a holiday playground and a haven for retirement from the smoky skies of industrial Lancashire. Down the banks of the Dee there is a subtle difference. You could hardly call this part pretty, but the character, the whole 'feel' of the coast has changed. It is very flat, very muddy, subject to silting, dismal in bad weather, unattractive pictorially all the time. Apart from the background of hills on the west you might think we are back where we started: the Severn Estuary and the Monmouthshire shore all over again. But that is not so. The Severn goes by swirling strongly, an angry river, but the Dee, much shorter than the Severn, a really beautiful stream in its upper reaches, indeed for most of its length, is slower and lazier and brings down a lot less water, though, from appearances, nearly as much mud.

The Monmouth shore generally is a lonely one. Flint, after Glamorgan, has been the most industrialised county in Wales and the most densely populated. Road and railway run in company straight up the coast. On the Monmouth shores you could spend a day and not see a soul; on the Flint coast there are at least three large towns—Flint, Prestatyn and Rhyl—to say nothing of some smaller ones. There is plenty of company. The Romans came to mine for lead, and it is possible that minerals were worked even before they came. Since their times the county has produced lead, zinc, coal and iron, while the manufactures in centuries nearer our own days include steel, textiles, paper, bricks and chemicals. Some of these, coal especially, were in the south of the county, but those in the north were mainly near the Dee. And on the Dee were the ports from which the products were exported. Some goods went by road, perhaps, but roads were bad, while water transport was cheap; so water transport was used. The chief harbours were at Bagillt, Mostyn, Flint and Connah's Quay. In very early times ships came right up to the walls of Chester, which was regarded as the port for Ireland.

Silting of the estuary has always been a problem, and Chester ceased to be useful as a port centuries ago. As an alternative a quay was built at Shotwich in 1560 and was considered so important that a collection was taken in all churches in the kingdom to help to pay for it. Now Shotwich in its turn is a few miles from the shore.

Changes in the Dee Estuary have been taking place constantly, and they have taken place over a long period. It is hardly possible in a few words to give a simple picture of all that has gone on, especially as the changes take place all the time. On the one hand the mud comes down river without ceasing, and on certain tides sand comes in. On the other hand much reclaiming of large areas has gone on, so that what was shallow foreshore or marsh became valuable fertile land. Speed's seventeenth century map shows a different coastline from the one we know: opposite Holywell and Bagillt it is almost a mile further out. At Prestatyn it is nearer two miles north. The estimated second century coastline was further out still. It is possible, if the latter is anywhere near accurate, that the Dee came down a central channel through what is now estuary, though even then the land on each bank would have been very low and probably marshy.

Some of the changes could be due to loss of, or removal of forest. Flint county was once almost covered by dense forests. When Edward I came this way he brought men from the Forest of Dean to help clear a way through them. There are still some fine woods and plenty of lovely trees, but it is no longer a densely afforested area. I do not know a lot about the submerged forests on this coast, but I was shown a photograph of one off the Cheshire side, and there are the bases of trunks and the strongly spreading buttresses of surface roots. My immediate impression was that it was a picture of trees that had been cut down. Now, as most people know, nothing can alter a countryside so surely as removing forests. When the trees go all sorts of strange things take place, from changes in the water table to dustbowl conditions.

The converse can happen. I have seen a documentary film which showed how at some place on the coast of Scotland the sanding up of a wide foreshore was arrested by tree planting, though getting trees to grow in difficult conditions is not nearly as easy as cutting them down.

If, at some time, forests grew as thickly along the coast as they did inland in the county, and if they died out or were removed, it may well be that it opened the way for the sand and the sea to move in. It is possible, and it would explain a number of things that at present do not seem to have any explanation.

One very pleasant feature about Flintshire is that very, very little of it is more than six miles from the sea. The furthest point away from the sound of the waves would be Mount Pleasant in the south, which would be ten miles or so from Connah's Quay as the crow flies. Using country lanes you could add half on to that. Another good characteristic is that the mines and manufactures have hardly affected the countryside at all. You can stand among all the hideous impedimenta in which manufactures clothe themselves, yet ten minutes walk away you can be in as beautiful countryside as you will find anywhere along the border. Mostyn Quay with chimney stacks and railway wagons and some tumbledown buildings is frankly ugly, but Mostyn Hall, where Henry Tudor escaped from his enemies by jumping out of the window as they came through the front door, stands in its wooded grounds as serene a stately home as you could find anywhere. Though you could put four Flintshire hills on top of each other and hardly reach the summit of Snowdon, some of them are quite high, varying from Hope Mountain, which is 1,080 feet, to Moel Fammau, Mother of Hills—a lovely title— nearly 2,000 feet.

Rhyl practically rules the north coastline. In 1914 with a popu- lation of over 13,000 it was a few hundred less than Llandudno. Today Llandudno's 16,500 is nearly 5,000 less than Rhyl. Not that population matters, and it is hardly likely that holiday-makers compare populations before deciding where to go. But both started from nothing, and a century ago, they say, there were only two cottages where Rhyl is now. Llandudno did at least have its inn.

Prestatyn, a few miles to the east, on the other hand, though as much in the tourist industry, has a long and honourable history, and all kinds of prehistoric relics have been found in the neighbour- hood. The best known is the Prestatyn Lady, a very ancient lady, too, for she is the skeleton of a Neolithic woman that was found during some excavations in the High Street in 1924. There are graves dating from the Stone Age in the neighbourhood, and there is the site of Roman building near the golf course. Offa started his Dyke close to the town, and there was once a Norman Castle. Elizabeth I did not sleep here, but Charles II did, and that is the next best thing. Rhyl may have outstripped Prestatyn since, but we are not sure that it even had its two cottages when Prestatyn was entertaining royalty.

Towns come and go, but history is for ever, and a greater place than either of the resorts completes a triangle south of Rhyl. At Rhuddlan history was made. It was an important town when its great castle dominated the marsh where the Saxons defeated the Welsh, as mentioned earlier, in 796. In those days the Clwyd was possibly wider, certainly deeper, and ships came up to Rhuddlan's quays.

Giraldus and Archbishop Baldwin stayed a night in 1188: "We arrived at Ruthlan, a noble castle on the river Cloyd belonging to David, the eldest son of Owain, where at the earnest invitation of David himself, we were handsomely entertained that night."

Edward I built the present castle, and his daughter Elizabeth was born in it. In 1283 Edward called a parliament to Rhuddlan. They met in Parliament House, still to be seen in the street, and in 1284 came the Statute of Rhuddlan. This is chiefly noted for its settlement of the six counties, as they were then: Anglesey, Cardigan, Merioneth, Carmarthen, Cardigan and Flint. But it was in reality an Act which annexed Wales to England and decided how the country was to be governed. Though many of the ancient Welsh laws were included in the Statute, there were some English ones as well, and for that harsh and lawless age some of them were good ones. An example of new rules, which had to be enforced by the sheriff, was the one dealing with "thieves, manslayers and other malefactors".

When those wrongdoers fled to the church for sanctuary

the coroner, as soon as he shall be certified thereof, shall direct the bailiff of our lord the king for that commote to cause to come before him at a certain day the good and lawful men of the neighbourhood; and in their presence, after recognition made of the felony, shall cause the abjuration to be made in this manner: That the felon shall be brought out unto the church door, and a seaport shall be assigned him by the coroner, and then he shall abjure the realm; and according as the port assigned shall be far or near, the term shall be set for his going out of the realm aforesaid: So that in journeying toward that port, bearing in his hand a cross, he shall not in any manner turn out of the king's highway, that is to say, neither upon the right hand nor upon the left, but shall always hold to the same until he shall depart the realm.

The castle stood strongly, guarding its little town until the Civil War, when the inevitable slighting took place after it was captured by Colonel Mytton. Today, in comparative ruin, it looks formidable, and there is still a nobility in its decay.

South of Rhuddlan is St. Asaph, little more than a typical Welsh market town, yet a city, since it has a cathedral. The cathedral began as a monastery in the sixth century, and at one time there were 1,000 monks, which is nearly half the present total population. There is a story that the monks were divided into three, and always one third was at worship so that at Llanelwy (the original name) the praise of God went on continually day and night.

The history of this little city is centred round its cathedral, and many famous names, both English and Welsh, are associated with it. Geoffrey of Monmouth was its bishop from 1152 to 1154, and they say he was ordained only a fortnight before his consecration. Geoffrey's *History of the Kings of Britain*, is about the most unreliable history ever written—but how much more interesting than the accurate ones! As mentioned earlier, it was certainly instrumental in getting the Arthurian legend started, and though that is poor history it is wonderful myth.

William Morgan, who translated the Bible into Welsh, was a bishop of St. Asaph. He and seven other men who had translated some of the Scriptures at one time or another are commemorated in the memorial facing the High Street.

The vestry contains a small but interesting museum. Among objects of interest in it are the manuscript of Dic Aberdaron's Hebrew-Greek-Welsh dictionary, a Breeches Bible (Adam and Eve made themselves "breeches" instead of "aprons"), A Vinegar Bible (the Parable of the Vinegar instead of Vineyard), charred beams from the cathedral Glyndwr burned, old manuscripts, old Welsh and Manx Bibles and Prayer Books, a first edition of the Authorised Version of the Bible, autographs and some prehistoric and Roman remains.

Between St. Asaph and Abergele is Bodelwyddan, where there is a famous modern church. It is called the Marble Church, and, though it is white outside, the marble is inside the building, the exterior being of white limestone. It was built 1856-60 by Lady Willoughby de Broke as a memorial to her husband. The arcades of marble inside the church are impressive, while outside, from a distance, the white building and its tall, slim, tapering spire are even more impressive.

From Bodelwyddan it is only a short step to the sea again, but if you turn east towards the Dee estuary—and that is no great distance—you can, by taking a by-road, come to the village of Caerwys. The name must not be, as it sometimes is, confused with Caersws in Montgomeryshire, though they have this in common that Caersws was an important Roman station on the Caerleon-Segontium (Caernarvon) route, and many experts think that Varis, an outpost of Deva (Chester) was here. At any rate, Pennant found an upright stone with a Latin inscription on it in use as a gatepost on a Caerwys farm. It may still be in existence, for he had it removed to his home at Whitford.

Strictly speaking, Caerwys is not a village but a town. Long ago it was one of three places where a person could be judged according to Welsh law. Up to the sixteenth century, when they were moved to Flint, the assizes were held here. There were a town Hall, a jail and a place of execution.

Caerwys is best known for its associations with the eisteddfod. Some people think that the eisteddfod is fairly modern, but that is not so. As a means of competition in the arts, particularly in music and poetry, it is a very ancient institution. The ceremonial observed at the National Eisteddfod may or may not be as old, but most likely is not. What happened was that a Glamorganshire self-educated poet, Iolo Morganwg (David Williams), discovered, or professed to have discovered, various ceremonies of the druids that should be observed at eisteddfodau. I have been told he did this to revive interest in the eisteddfod at a time when it was in decline. The question of whether he did discover these ceremonies or made them up has waked up a hornet's nest on more than one occasion, but Iolo was an eccentric who did pass off some of his own poems as the work of earlier and more famous poets. As I would prefer that the hornets should not buzz round my head, I will quote Sir Leonard Davies and Averyl Edwards (*Welsh Life in the Eighteenth Century*). They said Iolo

did not hesitate to draw upon his own versatile genius when the fount ran short. His interpolations and fabrications have enormously complicated the work of students. . . . He was largely responsible for the confusion of Bardic lore, and the grafting of supposedly Druidical ceremonies on to the Eisteddfod.

Iolo, in spite of a few literary forgeries, appears to have been a delightful character. He composed a triad: "There are three things I do not want: a Horse, for I have a good pair of legs; a Cellar, for I drink no beer; and a Purse, for I have no money."

The funny thing is he did have a horse, though he did not ride it. It accompanied him on his journeys, following behind, and if Iolo went into a bookshop for an hour or so it would wait for him in the street.

The most famous eisteddfod held at Caerwys took place about the year 1100, and from that time on the bards used it as their head-quarters. By Tudor times the meetings had fallen on evil days: "Vagrant and idle psons, naming themselfs mynstrells, rithmors and barthes are lately growen into such an intolerable multitude."

The Tudors took an interest in Wales, as they should have done, being partly Welsh and owing their crown very largely to Welsh help. Elizabeth I sent instructions to Sir Roger Mostyn to organise an eisteddfod at Caerwys that should separate the bards from the rabble of would-be bards. The latter were to be ordered "that they returne to some honest labour and due exercise, such as they be most apte unto for mayntenaunce of their livings, upon payne to be taken as sturdy and idle vacaboundes, and to be used according to the lawes and statutes pvided in that behalf".

The meeting was held on 26th May 1568, and degrees were awarded for singing, for playing the harp and for playing the *crwth*. The *crwth* is now obsolete. I believe there are examples of it in the Folk Museum at St. Fagan's. It is doubtful if anyone can play it, though if it is true that what man has done man can do again, it should not be impossible to learn. It had six strings and was played with a bow and the thumb. It must have been a very difficult instrument; by 1770 only one man could be found in the whole of Wales who was able to play it.

Dyserth, to the north, and almost back on the coast again, is another ancient village-town that has seen great days in the past. The Romans are believed to have mined lead in the locality. Sometimes I wonder how those people used all the lead, for they mined it in many places all over Central Wales and North Wales. There was a strong castle at Dyserth from very early times, and no doubt it was enlarged and strengthened in Norman times since it would be a very useful strongpoint on the coast route. Leland has a story of one of its constables, Sir Robert Pounderling, who fought in a tournament with a Welshman. The Welshman knocked out one of Sir Robert's eyes. Later he offered the constable the chance of revenge in another tournament.

"No thank you," said one-eyed Sir Robert. "You might knock out the other."

As Falstaff said, "The better part of valour is discretion."

Strange how an odd little story like that will stay in the mind, yet I had forgotten that in 1261 Llewelyn ap Gruffydd took the castle and destroyed it—and how many of the defenders were allowed to practise discretion then?

I suppose we prefer to smile rather than to weep.

At Point of Air the coast sweeps round into the estuary. The Point is reached by the little road up to Talacre, though except for the lighthouse there is not very much to look at except the sea and, in clear weather, the ships going to or leaving the Mersey and Liverpool. As they would have written on an old map: *Here is solitude*, or, according to the writer's temperament, *Here is peace.* Llanasa is a mile or so south with Gronant Moor lying between it and the sea. The tradition is that at one time from Gronant Moor you could make yourself heard on the Cheshire side by shouting. A loud voice, you would think, looking at a map or staring across, but if the old maps were anything near correct the story may be true; Flint and Cheshire have no doubt been nearer at times than they are today. Llanasa is an old village with an old church (fifteenth century), old glass in it and an old pulpit. The village is a mile or so from the estuary and the main road along which the traffic hurries to Prestatyn or Rhyl.

The road by the shore is very straight now and as a rule very busy, and my own preference has always been to go down the little lanes, which are not very straight but also are not busy. Whitford is just south-west of Mostyn, and this is claimed to be the prettiest village in the county. That may well be so, but it has an even better claim to fame in the fact that it was where Thomas Pennant lived.

He lived at an old mansion called Downing Hall. It is a short distance from the village down a lane, or drive, from what we will call, by courtesy, the main road. He was born there in 1726. He was brought up in the old Welsh fashion by foster parents. In his case they were tenants of his father, and this upbringing did him much good for he grew up understanding another way of life besides that of a country gentleman. Eventually he went to Oxford, though he did not take a degree. He became interested in history, archaeology and natural history; he travelled and visited; he corresponded with Gilbert White of Selbourne and with Linnaeus. He wrote about his travels and what he had seen and observed. "The best traveller I ever read," said Johnson. "He observes more things than anyone else does." He published books on natural history and his travels, *A Tour of Scotland* being perhaps the most popular. *Tours in Wales* is the book that has been quoted here so often, and it is fascinating in that, besides what one may call his academic reports, he was always ready to side-track these to look more at human beings: a long pedigree, somebody of great age, the fasting woman at Barmouth, a cursing well at Llanelian and so on. I imagine that in modern times he would have made a useful journalist for he had a flair for finding good stories. As well as being something of a classical scholar, it is important to remember that, unlike most of his fellow squires, he spoke Welsh. Without that his *Tours* would not have been half as interesting as they are, since in his day many people in North Wales spoke only their own language.

He died at Downing in 1798 and was buried at Whitford.

The various objects of antiquarian interest, manuscripts, books and so on were kept at Downing and were known as the Pennant Collection. Unfortunately the house was burned down in 1920. I say "burned down", but when I went to look at it many years later the shell I saw was very like a photograph of it I had seen in a book published in 1914. In fact, from a distance it looked like a living house. Perhaps the fact that the chimneys stood and there were even a few roofs gave that illusion, but my impression was not of ruin. Only when I went nearer could I see roofless rooms, doorways with no doors, debris behind the walls, and trees growing inside and coming out through the glassless windows.

On his journeys he usually had the company of his friend John Lloyd, the rector of Caerwys, and indeed on some of the routes he rode over a little good company would not have come amiss. To complete the party he took a Whitford man, Moses Griffiths, who was a servant at Downing. This man was an artist. He was not educated, he was self-taught, but he certainly could draw. The engravings used as illustrations to the book are his work.

The drawings marked Moses Griffiths [wrote Pennant] are the performances of a worthy servant whom I keep for that purpose. The candid will excuse any little imperfections they may find in them, as they are the works of an

Rhuddlan Castle, Flintshire, and the River Clwyd from the west

untaught genius, drawn from the most remote and obscure parts of North Wales.

The apology was unnecessary. The engravings are as good as any I have come across in books of this nature, and better than many.

In Whitford parish there is a perfect tenth-century wheel cross. It is called the Maen Achwyfan or Stone of Lamentation, though what calamity it laments is not known.

A couple of miles away is Holywell, which is not far from the Dee between Greenfield and Bagillt. For centuries this was a centre to which pilgrims came, and it is doubtful if even St. David's had as many visitors as those who came here with their aches and pains, their diseases and infirmities and woes to beg for help at the holy well of St. Winifred.

In the seventh century lived a virgin of the name of Wenefrede, of noble parents; her father's name was Thewith, a potent lord in the parts where Holywell now stands; her mother's Wenlo, descended from an antient family in Montgomeryshire, and sister to St. Beuno. Beuno assumed the monastic habit, retired to Clynnog, in Caernarvonshire, where he built a church and founded a convent. After completing this work of piety, he visited his relations in Flintshire, and obtaining from his brother-in-law a little spot at the foot of the hill, on which he resided, erected on it a church, and took under his care his niece Wenefrede. A neighbouring prince of the name of Cradocus, son of King Alen, was struck with her beauty, and at all events determined to gratify his desires. He made known his passion to the lady; who, affected with horror, attempted to escape. The wretch, enraged at the disappointment, pursued her, drew out his sabre and cut off her head. Cradocus instantly received the reward of his crime: he fell down dead, and the earth, opening, swallowed his impious corpse.

The severed head took its way down the hill and stopped near the church. The valley, which, from its uncommon dryness, was heretofore called Sych nant, now lost its name. A spring of uncommon size burst from the place where the head rested. The moss on its sides diffused a fragrant smell. Her blood spotted the stones, which, like the flowers of Adonis, annually commemorate the fact, by assuming colours unknown to them at other times.

St. Beuno took up the head, carried it to the corpse, and, offering up his devotions, joined it nicely to the body, which instantly reunited. The place was visible only by a slender white line encircling the neck, in memory of a miracle, which surpassed far that worked by St. Dionysius, who marched in triumph after decapitation with his head in his hands, from Montmartre to St. Denis, or that of St. Adelbertus, who, in like circumstances, swam across the Vistula.

St. Winifred lived fifteen years after this, and after she died her bones were eventually taken to Shrewsbury. A bell there dedicated

Salmon fishing boats below the Old Dee Bridge

M

to her honour, when it was rung, "allayed all storms, diverted the thunderbolt; drove away evil spirits".

The well gave 2,000 gallons a minute, and after some miraculous cures became famous as a healing well. Rich and poor visited it, drank its waters and bathed in them in the hope of being granted ease from their sufferings. The well over the spring and the chapel were paid for by Margaret Beaufort, mother of Henry VII. Of course the Reformation reduced the number of pilgrims, but the theology of priests and kings does not stop sick people wanting to be made whole; they continued coming and they still come.

You don't hear so much today about miracles; perhaps if there were one we could find a computor that would explain exactly *how* it happened. But it is all very mysterious; a little faith goes a long way, I know, but take a look at the crutches and other cripples' aids that sufferers have left behind. Some of their owners may have only imagined they were the lame, the halt and the blind, with psychosomatic symptoms that they could have cleared up by autosuggestion—but not *all* of them surely.

Of Basingwerk Abbey, not far away, little is left now. It was one of the great Cistercian foundations in North Wales, and was noted for its hospitality. One of the bards said (in Welsh) that the Abbot gave twice the treasure of a king in wine alone, and he mentions sugar as one of the luxuries found on the table. In Pennant's day there were "considerable remains". The Mostyns had not long stopped using it as a residence, and a tanner was living in a part of it at the time of his visit.

There was a castle here also, built by Richard Lupus, Earl of Chester. This Richard made a pilgrimage to St. Winifred's Well but

was attacked by the Welsh and obliged to take shelter in Basingwerk. He applied to St. Werburg for relief; who miraculously raised certain sands between Flintshire and Wiral, and thus gave means to his constable to pass to his assistance: which sands, from that time were called the Constable's Sands.

Mold is much further south and much further inland, though not many miles from Connah's Quay, but I would not visit it now (apart from enjoying the tangle of lanes in Flintshire) were it not the birthplace of Daniel Owen. He was born in 1836, died in 1895, and was the first Welsh novelist of any stature. In fact he is nearly the only Welsh novelist, for, though Welshmen have written novels, nearly all have written in English. Daniel Owen wrote in Welsh only. Novels were by no means popular among his countrymen; some considered them downright wicked and inspired by the devil. So it was not an easy-money type of writing he chose, and the family was very poor, his father and two older brothers having lost their lives in a pit disaster. Exaggerated claims have been made for his place in literature, some of his readers claiming, for instance, that he was as good as Dickens; but from the little I know of his work (in translation) I consider he had at least a remarkable talent. His early days were spent as a tailor, and the old Welsh tailor, sometimes working in his shop, sometimes travelling from farm to farm to make clothes for an entire family saw and heard much of interest, and became, in the best sense of the word, a gossip. A shrewd observer could learn a lot about human nature.

Daniel Owen was such an observer, and what he learned of human nature he used in his novels. It is said that his Welsh was excellent. He was a good story-teller and he knew how to create character. The pictures he has left of the Welsh day-to-day life of his time are fascinating. Mold does well to honour him.

Hawarden, a short distance east of Mold, is remembered less for its castle, its sieges and the calamities of wars, than because it was the home for sixty years of William Ewart Gladstone.

Coming back to that miraculous path across the estuary, I have been told that many years ago—a century perhaps—it really was possible at low tide to walk across from Flint to Parkgate. At first that did not seem possible. The Dee is not a mighty torrent, but it is certainly not a river you could cross by paddling. But on second thoughts it did not seem so improbable. If a stream runs on to hard flat sand it seldom keeps inside one narrow channel when the tide is out. It spreads itself and flows, a few inches deep—say ankle-deep at the most—over a considerable width of sand. I remembered the little stream that divides Pembrokeshire from Carmarthenshire— a nice little trout stream, no Mississippi, but you could be up to your waist in it. Then it flows through the pebble ridge below New Inn, passes Black Rocks and spreads in the way I have described so that at low water you would hardly need to take off shoes and stockings to cross.

All the same I would prefer to get from Flint to Parkgate by road nowadays, even though it meant a few more miles, or wait until the tide was full and row across. If a mist came up quickly when the tide was coming in you could soon lose all sense of direction. I cannot quote any actual examples of people being drowned through trying for a quick short cut, but undoubtedly they have been. J. M. Edwards in his little book *Flintshire* wrote, "As we glance across we are deceived as to its width and many an unfortunate wanderer has met an untimely death through being caught by the tide on these trackless wastes."

The best-known tragedy is the one Charles Kingsley told in *The Sands of Dee*, once a popular selection for school reading books. His lines seem to capture the desolation that can fall on these shores in the wind and the mist. No doubt his poem about the girl, Mary, who was drowned when she went out on the wastes to fetch the cattle is based on fact.

> The creeping tide came up along the sand,
> And o'er and o'er the sand,
> And round and round the sand,
> As far as eye could see.
> The blinding mist came down and hid the land,
> But never home came she.

Kingsley claimed that Adam de Kyngeslegh who was constable of Flint Castle in the late fourteenth century was his ancestor.

A more important link with literature—or a link with more important literature—was through Edward King, who, when a young man, was shipwrecked and drowned on his way to Ireland from Chester in 1637. He was the friend of Milton, and Milton wrote *Lycidas* in his memory.

> He must not flote upon his watery bier
> Unwept, and welter to the parching wind,
> Without the meed of som melodious tear.

*Lycidas* is a much finer poem than *The Sands of Dee*, yet the latter, free of the involved classical allusions of Milton's poem, is the more moving.

Modern Flint is the centre of a lot of factories and mines, though few, if any, of the latter are still worked, and the district bears the scars of industry. These are comparatively recent wounds. In the seventeenth century a traveller complained, "They have no sadler, taylor, weaver, brewer, baker, botcher or button-maker; they have not so much as the sign of an ale-house." The last statement is hard to believe, for, however much modern manufactures try to hide the fact, this is an old town and always has been an important centre, partly because it linked up best with the Cheshire shore, by the reputed low-tide ford and by ferry. Pennant was sure the Romans were settled here, and if they were it may have been for the lead-mining. A number of Roman remains have been found in the neighbourhood.

It must have been important in the English-Welsh struggle, and the present castle was started by Henry II who, after a defeat among the forests and hills, always afterwards used the coast and the coast road. In its present form, Flint Castle was one of Edward I's string of fortresses. The town's first charter was granted in 1283. There is no other Welsh castle with Flint's peculiar construction of three corner towers and the other, larger one, apart from them; but the lay-out might have been copied from Lillebonne in Normandy, where the plan is similar.

Flint was a suitable and convenient starting point for many of the campaigns in Wales, but it is better remembered, through Shakespeare, as the place where Richard II gave up all hope and his kingship. He was tricked out of Conway, taken by his enemies at Penmaenrhos, finally humiliated at Flint.

He has never ranked as a great monarch, except on that one memorable occasion when he faced a London rabble after the death of Wat Tyler. But Fate seems to have treated him over-harshly.

At first Bolingbroke pretended Richard was still king and spoke humbly.

Henry Bolingbroke
On both his knees doth kiss King Richard's hand
And sends allegiance and true faith of heart.

Did he really say that? Or has Shakespeare so bewitched us with words that we can no longer distinguish history from poetry?

Froissart said that even Richard's dog deserted him. When the two men met the pet greyhound fawned on Henry.

Cosyn, quod the kynge, it is a great good token to you, and an evyll sygne to me. Sir, how know you that, quod the duke. I knowe it well, quod the kynge. The grayhounde maketh you chere this daye and kynge of Englande, as ye shalbe, and I shalbe deposed: the grayhounde hath this knowledge naturallye: therefore take hym to you: he wyll folowe you and forsake me.

Poor Richard! Not a good king, yet who could refuse pity to one who fell so low?

Up the estuary from Flint is Connah's Quay, that started long ago as Wepre, a name mentioned in Domesday Book. Under that name it can be found on old maps; under that name it grew up as an important Dee port. In the eighteenth century it was New Quay, and early in the nineteenth took the name of a local innkeeper and became Connah's Quay, which name can be found on an 1839 map.

The town lives on industry now, but if you look carefully you can see something of the ancient little seaport that was so useful in olden days to the trades of south Flintshire.

But the coast of Wales is not at an end yet, though only a few miles are left. Down to Queensferry and north again, and there lie the flat lands that are all Flint has on the north and east of the Dee.

There is little to see but the sand and the flat shores, little to hear but the sea birds and the wind on the water. It is strange to think that a few miles further on Birkenhead sprawls out into the peninsula, while, across the Mersey, Liverpool spreads itself out into Lancashire. And it is strange to think that these two were unimportant hamlets when the ships were sailing up and down the Dee and Flint was the meeting place of kings. Strange to think that the two giants struggled against the problem of silting, and won—and so became giants. While the Dee ports struggled against the problem of silting, and lost—and so became small towns, even villages, instead of cities, villages where you can still hear the voice of the water and the crying of seabirds.

It might even be that some future, wiser people than we are will say, not that they lost but that they won.

# INDEX